BALLOON
TO THE
MOON

BALLOON TO THE MOON

A GUIDE TO VIBRANT LIVING

RHÉGINA SINOZICH, MSW

Abrezia Press

No part of this book may be used or reproduced in
any manner whatsoever without written permission except in the case
of brief quotations embodied in critical articles and reviews. For information address Abrezia Press, PO Box 8129, Silver Spring, MD 20907.

FIRST EDITION

Publisher's Cataloging-in-Publication

(Provided by Quality Books, Inc.)

Sinozich, Rhégina
        Balloon to the moon — a guide to vibrant living /
    Rhégina Sinozich. — 1st ed.
    p. cm.
    Includes index.
    LCCN 00-192791
    ISBN 0-9706297-7-X

    1. Self-actualization (Psychology) 2. Motivation
(Psychology) 3. Spirituality.   I. Title

    BF637.S4S56 2001   158.1

                                        QBI01-700143

This book is printed on recycled/acid free paper

Cover designed by Robert Aulicino

For Maija & Sofi,
whose very
essences
embrace life —
may your inner fires always
burn so brightly.

CONTENTS

ACKNOWLEDGEMENTS

To Maija Rejman—who wore all kinds of hats during the writing of this book. Thank you from the bottom of my heart for your love, support, sense of humor and vision. Life just wouldn't be the same without you!

To Conni Sinozich—who taught me that I can do anything I set my mind to.

To the memory of John Sinozich, Jr.— who taught me that time is precious and life is short.

To Dottie Podgorny for those wonderful dinners replete with her seasoned wisdom.

To Carol Heil for believing in this project from the start, and her unfaltering support.

To Lois Rosen for her unabashed excitement.

To Joshua Goldstein for his "insider" view of book publishing.

To Sofi Sinozich for running the press, and for her contagious enthusiasm about "Mom's book."

To Kismet, Sheba and the Breeze for keeping my feet warm and my heart open.

And last but not least, to *all my clients* for opening your hearts and lives to me. I continue to stand in awe of your processes and feel deeply honored to be a part of them. You are my greatest teachers. This book would not have been possible without you.

(1)

The Invitation
A Call to Authenticity

REGARDLESS OF WHAT IS HAPPENING IN OUR LIVES, each and every single day brings a kaleidoscope of opportunity. So let's embrace the possibilities. Let's paint our lives with brilliant palettes of colors, flinging paint onto our canvases with freedom and joy.

We all have within us phenomenal raw potential which is meant to be realized. Our inherent notes yearn to create symphonies of exquisite beauty. Let's become the brilliant beings we are meant to be.

We are part of a tremendous body of cosmic energy. The energy that bursts a flower open in springtime, that orbits masses of planets around each other, that crashes waves to shores, permeates our beings. We have access to the same impetus a seed uses to become a daffodil, a body uses to grow fingers and develop features.

Our universe is overflowing with this creative power. It

is infinite, and it is ours for the taking. This energy flows freely and easily. When the time is right, a tree bursts into flower, grows leaves, and bears fruit. We get our "stuff" from this endless pool of creative juice. It does not matter if we are arguing a case in court, scaling a mountain wall, or painting by a stream. The energy source is the same.

When we are open and receptive, we channel this energy. It courses through our beings and manifests in an endless variety of ways. When we move beyond our ego's boundaries and reconnect with the universe, the power and possibilities are tremendous. The puissance of the ocean, particularly the cosmic ocean we are made of, is mind boggling. Every living being is from and of this genius. Below the surface, beneath the layers of protective coating we amass, we are one. When we pour ourselves, boundless, back into the ocean of universal creativity, we become one with it. Its power is of us. We ignite our full vibrancy, expanding toward full capacity; we dip into the realm of pure potentiality.

When we are connected to the universe, when we are open and accepting, anything is possible. This is the place where miracles happen, where our dreams manifest.

We are meant to be fully active co-creators in the masterpieces that are our lives. We are meant to be dynamically imaginative and creative.

The basic principle is a simple one: if we stay connected and are true to ourselves, we will prosper. Staying connected is not so easily done for many of us. The further we grow beyond the womb, the more challenging it becomes to maintain an open channel with the infinite. The world seems to conspire against our being true to who we are. We are told how to act. We are defined by parents, siblings, teachers, lovers and friends. We internalize these things, losing track of our own internal voice, our internal guide. We feel confused and lost. We wonder why we feel depressed and apathetic, even as we achieve more and more of our dreams. We wonder why we do not feel free.

We have to be fully present in the moment to appreciate what is coming our way. It has to be what we really want, what our core beings want—not what we have learned we should want, or even necessarily what everybody else wants—and, we have to be authentic, fully ourselves. We have to be completely alive to really feel what is happening to us. We have to return to our senses.

It is not easy to be our true selves. Over generations, we have moved away from our authenticity and aligned ourselves with our adjusted selves, with our egos. We forget who we are. We get bogged down by old issues. We chase after "outside" things—"outside" achievements hoping for fulfillment. We get trapped in the dance of the ego and disconnect from our internal, spiritual eyes, from our true selves. And as we disconnect, we lose access to the universe and its infinite energy.

We have but to look at consumerism to understand the lure of the false self. Ego rules in this arena. The line is if "You have ____ you will be ____." Fill in the blanks with beautiful, rich, sexy, etc. It is the illusion of the quick fix.

The irony is that ____, when used as a quick fix, takes us further and further away from the real fix, which is our true self. We already have this. We do not need to buy it. We do not even need to borrow it. It may be buried and dormant, but it is inside each and every one of us, yearning to thrive. It can never be lost, and we have but to call on it for it to reappear in our lives.

This separation from our true selves, from the infinite, creates an inconsolable void and a tremendous amount of fear. From this place, nothing is as it should be. We look for safety in conformity. We follow the rules. We become uncomfortable with differences that deviate too far from our "norm," and thus the legacy gets passed on from generation to generation.

As children, we get strong and clear messages about conforming. We learn that we should sacrifice our true selves in order to "make it." We learn that our very survival conflicts with self-actualization. It is an either or scenario. For instance, when choosing a career, we are taught to be practical. "What will pay the bills?" Most of us are never asked, "What do you love to do?" "What brings you joy?" or "What gifts do you have to offer the world?" So, we lose the thread of our own stories. We arrive in adulthood with compromised access to our true selves, and thus to the creative force that permeates the very air we breathe.

How to regain access to our authentic selves is a vital question because all other questions spring from it. Without our true selves, we have nothing. We lose our vibrant core. We lose our drive and our inherent joie de vivre. We lose our compasses.

Life has a way of callousing us. It is hard to feel our way through a dark labyrinth with roughened senses. Some of us lose our fields of vision, our touch, our sense of direction—missing many of life's most exquisite landscapes.

This book is about finding ways to dissipate the callouses and heal them. It is about returning our selves to their intended states—states in which all six of our senses are fully alert. We will feel summer breezes and be moved by them. We will hear birds sing with our whole beings, and we will feel the excitement of doing what we are meant to do in this lifetime. We will embrace our lives and turn ourselves over to the giddiness left in the wake of this embrace.

This is a personal journey. It is a quest for authenticity and pure energy. And like all quests, it will include tears and hard passages. It will also include uncontrollable laughter and joy. For life, fully lived, is all of these things.

A journey to recapture the essence of our true selves inevitably becomes a journey of soul, of spirit. We cannot dive into the ocean of all possibilities without touching the divine, without reconnecting with infinity.

This book is about bringing out the light that lives in all of us, and protecting it so that it burns brightly. We are meant to bask in its glow, letting it shine forth. This light is contagious. It is our birth right.

We will work our selves like the soil on our land, creating fertile ground where the seeds of our dreams can grow profusely and abundantly. We will reopen the great pipelines to the source and let cosmic energy flood into our lives. We will burst through the glass ceilings we have unconsciously imposed upon ourselves.

All any of us needs for this journey is an open mind, a willingness to explore, and a balloon.

(2)

The Lens
Our Window to the World

OUR SELF, AS WE THINK OF IT IN THE HERE AND NOW, is the
container, the vessel that is available to us in this lifetime.
We live in it, travel in it and judge the world by what we
see and feel as we look out through its windows. We
channel our energy through it—our creativity, our life's
desires.

This great vessel of ours is made up of our body,
mind, and emotions. It forms the lens of our existence
and profoundly affects what we see, how we respond, and
what we create. Every detail of our lives comes to us fil-
tered through this lens. A clear, open lens brings in a different spectrum of light and color than a scratched,
cloudy one.   The aperture determines the kind of access
we have to the higher realms of our self. It opens our spir-
its to the ocean of all possibilities. When our lens is flung
open wide, it allows light into our lives. It is our conduit
to the creative genius of the universe.

We tend to focus on *what* we see, *what* we feel, rather than how we see, how we feel. We do not question the validity of what we take in. We assume the content is factual. It does not occur to us that our view of the world may be warped. It is easy to be unaware of the power these perceptions have in our life.

Our lens is a composite of our life experiences. It was formed over many years. Our emotional and biological predispositions, our childhoods, and the karma we carry from previous lives all influence who we become.

We come into this life closely aligned with our higher self. When we are parented by those who are also aligned with their higher selves, we continue to be real. Our connection to our higher self is maintained, and we develop authentically. We feel free to express ourselves in endless ways. We are actualized.

Most of us were not parented in this way. Some of us were lucky enough to have had some experience with this kind of parenting, others were not so lucky. With pressures from family and society, we begin, very early on, to adjust ourselves. We smother some of our desires, let go of some of our dreams. We develop masks to hide behind, and present false personae to the world.

We internalize the parenting styles of our caretakers, and in adulthood, these become our self-care styles. As we mature, we continue to parent ourselves with these learned styles, which perpetuates childhood legacies that might be better left behind.

A false self is dishonest, albeit unintentionally dishonest, and when we carry falseness in parts of ourselves, we are burdened with excess. It takes a great deal of energy to maintain a lie. Truth, on the other hand, sets us free. Only with honesty can we find our true self—our peace.

Our authentic self flows from our higher self. Our inauthentic self flows from our ego. Our ego keeps us agitated about things that do not matter, which can leave us feeling depressed, anxious, aggressive or lethargic.

Our false self requires an overactive ego with an entourage of half truths and lies to maintain its façade. Our ego keeps us looking in the wrong direction, it warps our view of life. It keeps our lens so muddied that we cannot see clearly.

Our ego thrives on fear and separation. It thrives on comparison and competition. It convinces us that we are "better," "worse," or "different" from everyone else—which leaves us feeling fundamentally alone, at odds with the world. We are left judging and feeling separate, lonely to the core. Our energy gets pulled away from the only life that can bring us genuine excitement and joy—life springing from our true source.

Judging works for our egos; it does not do a thing for us. Whether judging is aimed at ourselves or others, it is like smearing the paints on our palette, and then trying to create something splendid out of the mess we are left with. Ultimately, it does nothing but take away from the beauty of the picture we could have created.

When we are living from our ego, we do not have access to divine creativity. We are operating from a small glass of ocean water instead of diving, unbound, into that cosmic ocean of all possibilities. We are not reconnecting with all that is. We are painting with one color. On some level, this is an excruciating way to live. Our birthright is a place of boundless potential. Living from our ego, from our false self, leaves us focused on what is false. We are caught up in illusion, unavailable for what is real.

As adults, we are often living in an internal environment where we are not available to ourselves. It's a bit like parents who are so focused on the outside appearance of things that they cannot just be with their children. They cannot go to a ball game and have fun. We see them comparing their sons or daughters to others; we feel their judgment. They are not available to their children or to themselves.

The energy generated by judgment is extremely constricting. And it is no less powerful for us as adults, simply because the scene is played out internally. The path of the false self and the ego leads nowhere. It simply takes us further away from genuine satisfaction and peace. And the further away we get, the more adamant our ego becomes that its way is right. The criticism of others, the self aggrandizement or annihilation, merely grows as our ego tenaciously tries to maintain its hold on us.

Judgment is based on fear and inadequacy. None of us are inadequate. We are all made of the same stuff. We ultimately have access to the exact same ocean of possibility. Just because some of us are not tapping into that ocean at this moment does not make us less adequate. Judgment, and the climate of fear it creates, serves only to strengthen our ego and weaken our access to our higher self. It makes it impossible for us to fully use our resources to get on with the business of our life.

There are no shortcuts to honesty. It takes honesty to

create honesty. We need to consciously choose truth. Without truth, there can never be peace within us, for our life force will continue to be drawn away from us in the service of our ego's meaningless quests.

If we are to free ourself and live vibrantly in the moment, one of our tasks must be to look closely at our lens and seek out the ways in which it distorts our reality. We are genuinely happy and content, even through the hard times, when our lens is clear and we are living through our higher self rather than our ego. We feel guided and supported. When we are operating from our true self, life makes sense. We are able to handle what comes our way. The less genuine we become, the further we move from our source, from pure energy. Somewhere inside, we feel lost and lonely. We try to fill the void. We watch others, take in the messages of our culture, drink, smoke, shop, overeat, become addicted to relationships. All of this leads us further and further away from authenticity and happiness. We cannot live in the moment when we are chasing after "cures." And the moment is absolutely all we have.

(3)

It's 8 O'clock
Do We Know Where Our Beliefs Are?

OUR BELIEFS COLOR OUR LIVES. They create our stories. They determine whether we are just getting by; whether life is a lot of hard work and then we die; or whether life is a magical, mythical quest filled with awe. We build our lives belief-by-belief. Our realities come to life one thought at a time. Our beliefs determine where we move our cameras and what filters we use. They determine where we put our focus and how our narrator interprets the scene.

This point was poignantly driven home for me some ten years ago. I marched in a demonstration on Capitol Hill that was positive and invigorating. I was surrounded by energetic people, and we were all filled with optimism and hope. We felt a part of the process and really believed we were making a difference.

23

At one point during the demonstration there was a small counter-demonstration involving a handful of people. Tempers flared, and somebody was restrained and escorted away by police. That night, I watched the news on television, and I think my jaw actually dropped open while I sat there and stared at the screen. I could not believe what they were showing. The demonstration looked like an angry mob out of control. The cameras were angled to maximize the violence. There were no shots of the majority of the crowd, nor was there any mention that this was an incredibly positive, peaceful demonstration. The news media was not lying outright, but this was a totally inaccurate portrayal of that demonstration. It did not even graze the truth of that day.

The storyteller has such power. And we have that same power. We also carry this subjective power within ourselves. How we perceive things, where we aim our cameras, what lenses we use, what story lines we hand our narrators all have a powerful impact on our reality. It becomes our reality. We create our realities.

Great wads of stimuli bombard us all the time. It would be overwhelming but for the fact that our brains go to work for us and focus on certain things to the exclusion of others. As we walk down the street, we take in certain information, screen out other stimuli. Our beliefs tell our brains what to seek out. They are the directors of the movies of our lives. They tell the camera crews what to look for and where to look. The camera crews oblige by producing a movie completely consistent with the original script. Thus, we feel validated in our beliefs; we feel that our views are "correct." But our camera crews could just as easily have documented a script of polar opposite content.

We unconsciously look to support our beliefs. If we are convinced the world is a horrible place where people do horrible things, our brains will oblige and bring us a plethora of information supporting that belief. We will review the "facts," conclude that our original belief was correct, and our belief that the world is a horrible place is further strengthened. If, on the other hand, we believe the world is a good place where people are basically good, our "camera crews" will find different kinds of evidence for us. We will again see the "facts," and our belief that the world is a good place will be reinforced. Our beliefs self-perpetuate.

What do you believe? What are your core beliefs? What drives you? Do you believe people are inherently good or evil? Do you believe life is hard? Do you believe you deserve to be happy? Do you deserve to suffer? Allow your imagination to carry you away here. Open the gates and let some of these beliefs out into the light of day.

Our beliefs are not monsters that lurk deep within the unconscious realms of our beings. We have, however, often relegated them to an automatic pilot status. We do not think about them at all. But our beliefs are powerful, and it is crucial for us to take a look at them. We need to make sure that they are up to date, that they are reflecting the type of life we want to live. Our beliefs lead to our reality, our affectional experience of life. They are our "directors," our "scripts."

We can have conflicting beliefs sitting side-by-side, and this leads to stress and discomfort, like earthen plates grating against each other in opposite directions. Our creative flow is hampered—dampened at best, totally blocked at worst. We have control over our beliefs. They are nothing more than arbitrary thoughts, and as such, can be changed with attention, time and perseverance. Look at your life. How does it feel? This is the outward expression of your beliefs. The belief is the origin of the intent, then the camera crews bring in the evidence. Our storyteller interprets it in a certain way, and we react. We have feelings about what is coming in. Our emotions charge the data, flesh it out for us, make it real. It becomes life as we experience it.

The "data," per se, is irrelevant; it does not matter. That is how it is possible to have people who seem to have it all, yet are miserable and toxic. This is also how it is possible to see people who are barely surviving on a practical level, yet are filled with joy and love. The energy they emit is different and perhaps incongruent from what we would expect to see based on "outward" appearances.

The power is in the process of our lives. The content is irrelevant. It does us no good to have millions of dollars if we "feel" poor. If we feel poor our reality will be that we do not have enough. On the other hand, a hundred dollars in the bank can feel like a fortune if that is the story line our director decides to push.

We can determine if a belief is serving us by looking at how it leaves us feeling about ourselves. Is this a belief that opens our hearts, that expands us? Or, is it one that leaves us feeling constricted and ill at ease? A belief, such as "life is just a chore," may lead to us feeling perpetually tired and placid, dispassionate about our lives. Work feels hard from this place, like a constant uphill battle. Our health will not be vibrant or sound. Our energy will be low.

We are not at the mercy of our environment for our set of beliefs. Our environment is created by our beliefs, not the other way around. It is relative and personal. What we believe determines what we take in. And what we take in, we process as fact. It is not fact, but rather a subjective view. It is a self fulfilling prophecy. We get what we look for. And when we get what we look for, albeit unintentionally, and react to it, it further amplifies and solidifies our certainty that reality is a certain way.

Since we have some choice in the matter, we might prefer to feel that the world is a good place where bad things can happen, as opposed to a bad place where good things can happen. When we walk through our days gathering documentation on what a good place the world is, our batteries are recharged. We feel positive. We feel alive and vibrant. When we do come across the "bad" things in life, as inevitably we will, we will actually have some energy that has the potential for healing.

In the alternate scenario, when we walk through our days feeling bad about the world, our energy is constricted. We feel negative. When we come across something positive, we cannot really take it in. We are too antipathetic, too burned out and jaded.

We need to pay attention to our beliefs and how we describe the world to ourselves. We also need to pay attention to what we are focusing on in the world. There are infinite possibilities at any moment. We are not meant to take in, uncensored and unprocessed, great quantities of negativity. It needs to be processed, and rendered digestible if we expect to continue to operate at full steam. There needs to be some sense to the madness, some light. If not, our souls wither.

It is our responsibility to pay attention to what our psyches are choosing to focus on, what they are taking in. Never before in the history of the world have we had such access to information. It is a veritable smorgasbord. And it can be a dangerous place when not carefully and astutely navigated. We are bombarded with information on all fronts. The world is literally a fingertip away. Therefore, we are being called upon to process more information than ever before. The intellectual and emotional life of a seven year old in America today is more challenging than that of a fifty seven year old a century ago. Like galloping on an out of control horse, it can be a terrifying experience if we do not pull in the reins. Many of us have gone numb. We have become addicted to the incessant stream of stimuli from television, radio, newspapers, computers, billboards, and neon lights. We have desensitized ourselves by overloading ourselves.

We cannot just numb out one part of ourselves. When we turn the volume down in one area of our lives, we turn it down across the board. Our intentionality helps us use information precisely rather than letting the age of information stampede over our foreheads.

We live in wealthy times. The knowledge base is an incredible gift if we use it wisely. We can partake of this glorious feast purposefully, paying attention to our own individual temperaments. We can choose the dishes we sample carefully, and take time to digest and enjoy them.

We can pay attention to ourselves as we dine. Knowing the risks of overindulgence, we can be aware of the warning signs of overexposure. How are we witnessing this information? How is it leaving us feeling? We can also notice the process and respond. When we watch an incredibly violent scene on screen, or witness a caustic exchange on the street between strangers, we can pay attention to how we are responding. We do not need to clutter ourselves with unprocessed stimuli, or fortify beliefs that are damaging to the free expression of ourselves.

The tapestries of our lives are intricately woven. We need to choose our fabrics and thread with care. We need to weave with intentionality and mindfulness. We want to create an optimum internal environment, an ambiance in which our psyches will flourish.

29

④

The Emotional Caches
How Much Have We Tucked Away?

IN CHILDHOOD, WE BEGIN TO COLLECT DATA ABOUT THE WORLD. We cry; mommy comes; she holds us and says sweet things to us; she sings us a lullaby. We feel that the world is a good place. A cache is opened deep in the forest of our minds.

This scene is played out many times in our lives. Our "The world is a good place" cache fills, and as it fills, its magnetism increases. As information comes at us, if it is ambiguous, it will be drawn into our "The world is a good place" cache, further reinforcing that belief. Thus, some of our caches grow exponentially.

Obviously, all caches are not so positive. Many have headings like "Nobody loves me," "I don't deserve anything," "I'm not good enough," or "The world is a bad

31

place." The beliefs that drive these kinds of hideaways will wither our hopes for self-actualization.

Our dominant caches are overly active and powerful. They are charged with energy and are highly magnetic. They draw experiences and interpret them as supporting the beliefs they purport. If we have a cache that holds an "I'm no good; nobody loves me" belief, then whenever something comes our way that even remotely matches this belief, it will be drawn in and processed as "I'm no good; nobody loves me," further reinforcing that belief.

These caches are storehouses for unprocessed emotions. When all is well and we are living in a fluid way, without any backlog, we process life as we live it and our emotions do not get stuck.

Children are supposed to get help from their parents when life is difficult. Their caretakers support them as they process their sadness, disappointments, and rages. But it is not a perfect world, and many of us did not get the help we needed as children. Unprocessed issues are meticulously tucked away one at a time until we are left with some very oversized caches.

Once we have a backlog in a certain area of our lives, everything that comes along behind it is denied passage. Like pipelines with finite widths our caches can hold some unprocessed experiences, yet allow others to pass through for a time. But eventually, as more and more unprocessed material gets stuck, the flow stops and incoming feelings are trapped in the emotional excess of our caches. When we add things to negatively charged caches, content is stirred, and leftover emotion flares.

So, let's say we are buying some oranges at a local grocery store, and the cashier growls at us for not properly marking the bag. If we have a large "I'm no good; nobody loves me" cache, this experience will likely get pulled right into it. This upsets the emotional memories stored in this cache, and there we stand, flooded with all kinds of feelings that really have nothing to do with the unpleasant cashier or the oranges. The cashier's comment is just the trigger.

Our unprocessed emotions are ripe, and they explode with all their fetid intensity into our realities at the worse times—in the middle of a job interview, during a romantic dinner, on a fourteen hour plane trip.

The feelings, not coming with tidy little explanations of how the present situation reminds us of something in the past, often leave us dumbfounded and stunned. Not realizing what has just happened, we feel bombarded with emotion. We feel like we are five years old again, filled with shame and feeling that nobody loves us. Intellectually, we know that the cause of our feeling is absolute nonsense and has no basis in reality. Yet this emotional tidal wave feels totally legitimate and insurmountable. We watch ourselves spiral deeper and deeper into it, feeling helpless to stop the emotional deluge.

An alternate set of beliefs would have led our narrator to tell us a different story—which, in turn, would have been processed differently, perhaps not activating any leftover feelings. In the above example at the grocery store, we could have just decided the cashier was having a bad day. Not taking in the negative attitude, we would have been able to maintain a clear boundary around ourselves. The cashier's crankiness would have bounced right off.

Our early lives are so important in that they start us down the road to our beliefs. Our childhood caches stay fairly intact, continuing to grow, until something of magnitude happens in our lives to shake them up. Because of the energy and magnetism stored in our caches, we are drawn to using certain lenses, much as a record gets stuck in a groove that is worn over time. As with a stuttering record, we can choose a different track. We can move the needle. We can react when our record continues skipping over the same spot. Our awareness and attention are keys to self-actualization and the freedom it brings. We can consciously decide to change our beliefs.

Beliefs are powerful bastions of our internal landscapes. They are the colors we squeeze onto our palettes as we paint our lives. Numerous books tell us to just change the way we think and we will change our reality. That is true; it is that simple, but it is not that easy.

Beliefs are thoughts charged with emotion, memories, and evidence that prove them to be infallibly correct. Our negative beliefs carry unprocessed material, and unprocessed emotion. And like undigested food, this causes trouble. It clogs things up; it sours; it saps us of our energy.

Challenging our outdated beliefs risks unleashing difficult emotional energy. Parts of ourselves keep us held back, scared of that. Feelings that are not processed get frozen in time. Our beliefs affect what we look for. Our caches affect where that information goes internally, and what emotions get stirred up.

Information comes at us from the world. Our narrators interpret it for us, and this, in turn, triggers an emotional response. If a cache of unprocessed emotion is triggered, then we are likely to end up with a greater or lesser explosion seemingly erupting out of nowhere. The camera and the lenses affect how we process information that comes from the outside. The emotional wash, the hues of the painting, come from the inside. When our narrator passes a story along, it is labeled and drawn into a cache. It then evokes feelings stored in that cache. If the cache affected is a powerful one, we will have a strong reaction. If it is fairly benign, a fairly bland reaction will ensue.

When we are not cluttered with a backlog, our energy courses through the corridors of the incredible internal psychic houses that we are. Feeding on their own momentum, celebrating their own beings—our psyches dance on the turrets and balconies, dive into the pools, skip through the rooms, and tumble through the gardens of our inner space. When life's hardships come our way and we have the support—from our caretakers as children and from ourselves as adults—we process issues and our houses remain open and accessible. We may lose some of our vitality for a time, but we do not lose access to our houses. We remain fully alive.

If we do not have the support, if we are not able to process some of life's negatives—we begin to tuck emotional material away. Unprocessed hardships get shuttled away for safe keeping. As the rooms fill, we seal them off loosing our access to them. With each room we seal off, we lose a little more energy; we become a little more constricted until some of us find ourselves living out of a drab basement room.

The human psyche is an incredible thing. It is wonderful that we are able to compartmentalize and seal issues away. For trauma survivors, it was truly the only way to survive. It is the raft that has gotten many a child across viciously tumultuous seas into adulthood. But these rooms were only meant to be temporary holding grounds. The deal was "Okay, I'll hold this for you for awhile, but then you need to clear it out so we can use this energy again." Furthermore, these rooms have a half life. If we do not process the contents on our own, at some point in our adult lives, the walls of these rooms start to disintegrate and the contents begin to eke into our conscious lives.

We were never meant to live out of a drab basement room, and the universe reminds us of this. It rattles the doors. It nudges us. Every time we get broadsided with old emotional material, we are being provided with another opportunity to clear out the vestiges of our old caches and reevaluate our beliefs. Living from anything less than the whole house is intolerable, as is living with anything less than our inherent energy.

We are not meant to be prisoners of our life's unprocessed tragedies. Instead, we are meant to rise beyond the familial, societal, and cultural legacies that no longer work in our lives. We have all the keys we need to unlock the chains that hold us back from being fully actualized beings. We yearn for self-actualization, for our own expression of unbounded creativity, for that endless source that is our birthright. The song of the siren lures us to ever higher manifestations of our possible selves. The universe invites us constantly to authenticity.

The work we need to do to become freer is sometimes

difficult. We experience pain and sorrow, and we strive to get away from it, rather than letting ourselves move through it in order to reap the benefits of that journey. We are meant to engage our conscious selves to clear the path, to clean out any remnants that hamper our journey. We are meant to grow and evolve, striving not for perfection, but for authenticity and the bliss that this state brings. When we are real and open, when we are available, we have access to endless pools of energy, vitality, vibrancy, and creativity.

$\textcircled{5}$

Whose Movie Is This Anyway?
Taking Control of Our Scripts

WE HAVE A TENDENCY TO USE THE SAME CAMERA ANGLES, lenses and sound bites again and again. Much as a director who continues to do "takes" of the same scene, never quite getting it right, we will never get the finished feature we dream of when we operate from limiting beliefs. We tend to take a passive role in the editing of our movies, not realizing that we affect every aspect of our productions.

Beliefs are not meant to go unchallenged. We are not meant to have one set of beliefs to last a lifetime. When all is working well, we are constantly gathering new information and shifting our thoughts. We are auditioning new camera crews and experimenting with new angles, even though we may feel awkward, even scared.

We are willing to tolerate our vulnerability in order to stay fully alive. We greet life with hearts flung open wide.

We do not do well working from just one script. Instead, we change daily, and our scripts need to change with us. When we rework the same scripts, life loses its flare. We amputate our growth, we become disinterested and apathetic. We lose our inspiration.

We are meant to be inspired—"in spirit." When we are inspired, creativity flows through us, igniting our vistas with vibrancy and vitality.

The eye of the beholder is supreme. Outside events are unimportant. When we are "in spirit," we can look at the same landscape every day and be awed and moved by it. We can find solutions we never thought existed for challenges that have haunted us for years. Our state of mind creates our reality.

When we embroider our names on the director's chair, grab a megaphone, and pull up to the action—we become fully fledged producers of the show we call Our Lives. Our lives become meaningful and deeply attuned to our true desires. We regain our natural zest and enthusiasm for life.

⑥

Expanding the Container
Stretching the Border

OUR MINDS COMPOSE THE SYMPHONIES OF OUR LIVES. Our thoughts are the orchestras that bring them to life. We need to keep our instruments tuned; our rehearsals need to be regular. Like great conductors, we can pull tremendous potential out of our selves and bring it to fruition. We can train our minds to expand. We can turn them in the directions we want and broaden them. Our minds are what we feed them.

Modern technology has enabled scientists to study the human brain in amazing ways. We have discovered that in childhood, our brains grow exponentially. The ingestion of huge quantities of new information requires new neuropathways, and we literally grow our brains. New thoughts create new networks. The more we use our brains, the more complex and intricate they become. We need to make sure that our brains continue to grow in adulthood. We can deepen the scope of our minds with art, music, nature, literature, and challenging thoughts. When our minds grow we are using new cameras and lenses, writing new scripts, and reinvigorating our lives. Our self imposed boundaries evaporate when we daydream, as we stretch beyond the limits we have created. The more we use our minds, the more we expand them.

The external environment we select for ourselves, the internal scenery we create, one thought at a time, has a powerful influence on our lives. Like potent chemicals, our emotions wash across the landscapes of our realities, affecting our thoughts. Where we allow our minds to wander affects our feelings and our thoughts. Our feelings and thoughts feed off each other, creating an endless cycle. Thoughts alter feelings, feelings alter thoughts. We can, at any time, alter the predictable sequence of our thought/feeling pattern by actively challenging our thoughts and steering them in other directions. We can loosen their grip on our emotional state with humor.

Like quelling the bickering between musicians, we need to curb our own negativity; it distracts from the music. It is too easy to get caught up in day-to-day minutiae, letting ourselves simmer in pettiness for too long. We cannot leave our gardens to the weeds, for the possibilities of life are far too grand.

At times, we need to be like Ulysses, tying ourselves to the masts of our vessels to resist the songs of the sirens. Lures we need to watch out for are the songs of our egos and the inconsequential superficialities of our society.

The songs of these sirens sap our energy and distract us from meaningful existence.

Many of us go through life whistling the same tunes. We can consciously chose to expand at any time. We can listen to a piece of music, turn it up, hear it with our ears, tap it out with our feet, conduct it with our hands, dance it with our bodies, taste it with our mouths. We can cross modalities—listen with our fingers, hear with our mouths, feel with our eyes. Let's experiment. We can dance barefoot in a field and let a rainbow sweep us away. We can catch a raindrop on the tip of our noses and become that raindrop—whirling, dancing, and singing.

Let's extend ourselves and do something we have always wanted to do: rent a violin, hire a teacher, take a class; throw a pot, make some playdough; crank up the stereo and sing opera at the top of our lungs; ride a horse; climb a tree; or fly a plane. We expand when we play.

Can you remember how to finger paint? Can you go beyond worrying about what a mess you are making and turn yourself over to the moment, randomly smearing paint on paper? Can you forget about how silly you look and skip home from work one day? Can you take a couple of hours and give yourself permission to get absolutely nothing "productive" done? Can you wink at a stranger just because you feel like it? Can you draw something, not for the end result, but for the fun of it?

Let yourself get lost in your processes. Play the piano for the love of music, for the feel of the keys beneath your fingers and the resonance of the notes. Let go of your worries and let yourself be totally free—free of judgment, free of scrutiny, free of criticism.

As children in the orchestras of our lives, we play a little viola, some piano; we dabble with the drums; we take a whirl at conducting; we compose a few tunes. We move freely between roles, wearing many hats, not feeling compelled to chose one to the exclusion of the others. Why don't we reconnect with some of our possible selves, living from our full repertoire of possibilities? Every activity we have tried, and every dream we have dared to dream, leaves an imprint on our psyches. When we allow ourselves to call upon these dormant parts of our beings, we add tremendous depth and vitality to our lives.

Living from our full composite selves enriches our lives. Building layer upon layer, we create deeply fascinating, multi-dimensional beings to journey through life with. When we face challenges with our full orchestra, we get amazing results.

Perhaps we took a ballet class when we were younger, then dropped it. Perhaps somewhere inside of us, there is still a great love of ballet. Maybe we could reconnect with it, go to the ballet and let ourselves drink in the performance with all our senses. We could come home, put some classical music on, and dance—a pirouette, a jeté, a leap across the living room.

Does a good mystery rouse the great detective within? Can we imagine ourselves flying through space at the speed of light? Can we feel the imprint of a crown from some century long gone by? Let's play! Play and rekindle old sparks, rediscovering the fullness of ourselves. Let's invite all our possible selves into our daily lives, feeling the entourage of these wonderful fragments of ourselves, weaving them together into a whole, and becoming them all. We are so much more than we seem. Let's call upon the dancer when we walk, the singer when we write, the carpenter when we build. Let's break out of the compartments that have been internally and externally imposed upon us. Let's celebrate our multiplicity to the hilt, blur the margins, hold the whole, and stretch!

The children around us are masters at fluidity and expanded roles. They dance between roles, trying out various personas and beings, feeling free to express themselves in endlessly creative ways. Let's invite their energy into our beings and catch their joie de vivre, letting it infect us and reawaken within us our own eternal Pans.

Perhaps it is time to rediscover the whimsical fairies that live in all of us and summon them back into our lives. These elfin creatures know how to skip between the lines and move when we are convinced there is no place to go. They live in fantasy and know how to find the ridiculous in the overly serious.

Let's let ourselves be moved by the joy around us, the joy within us—finding reasons to smile and excuses to laugh, letting it roll out from deep within, allowing it to shake and rattle our very souls. Let's laugh until our sides ache and tears flow down our cheeks.

When pain knocks, let's not be afraid to open the door. Let's embrace our pain as we would any of life's other veils. We cannot live our lives deeply if we are only willing to fill ourselves with joy. We expand to accommodate what we are willing to take in—from darkness and from light. We inadvertently mute our capacity for joy when we anesthetize and numb our pain.

If we want to live fully, we need to let ourselves be touched by all of life's emotions, from the ecstacies to the agonies. We cannot have one without the other. There is no day without night, and no spring without winter. We need to let ourselves be touched by sadness, to allow ourselves to feel it, to cry, to weep, to be as open to it as we are to our laughter and our joy. We need to let it flow through us, to leave its mark upon us.

Through pain, we birth new selves and deepen our lives. We add rich textures to the fabrics of our experiences. Pain is opportunity. It renders us vulnerable; it flings open wide the windows of our psyches, expanding and transforming us. Pain renders us mutable, malleable. It deepens our containers, our selves, if we will let it.

In times of pain—though we are aware of the immediate crisis, the imminent sorrow or agony of a difficult passage—a parallel awareness of the deeper plane of our existence lends meaning and depth, creating profound opportunities for growth. A part of us can write the subtext, looking for the deeper level, never loosing sight of the mythic journey that our lives are. That part of us can look beyond the present, obvious angst and interpret the events from the perspective of the heroic quest we are each engaged in. Our pain is part of our search for authenticity and aliveness.

We do not get antiques without aging. The rugged cliffs of Normandy would not exist without years of Atlantic Ocean brutally meeting rock. We do not become rich, complex and soulful receptacles of life without living with profundity, accepting and embracing the positive and the negative in our lives. Our woundings are rites of passage. They are the sand that ekes depth out of our crucibles.

Pain, crisis, sorrow and illness are invitations into the depths. We come back from these adventures renewed, expanded, and recreated. They are invitations to partake in the treasures the oceans of our psyches hold for us.

Certainly it seems safer and easier at times to live a muted life. But it is not. Every time there is genuine angst in our lives, some fragment of our selves is trying to birth itself and evolve. Living in a muted state is a bit like trying to stop a psychic labor. It saps us of a tremendous amount of energy, leaving us flattened and dejected.

Living fully, drinking deeply from all the cups life offers us—her pain, sorrow, bliss, ecstasy, and blandness—gives us a full range of notes with which to compose the symphonies of our lives. When we mute ourselves, when we deprive ourselves of depth by not fully living, we create our life compositions with three notes. We live lives that feel tremendously lacking, and the bleak arrangements break our hearts. Intuitively knowing our true potential, we feel depressed and let down. Our cores yearn to create the full symphonic pieces they were born to execute on a daily basis.

⑦

Midwifing
Birthing New Selves

WE ARE CONSTANTLY REBIRTHING AND REMAKING parts of ourselves. As we grow and learn, old patterns of behavior no longer fit. Through pain, we shed the old and welcome the new.

My daughter is babysitting the kindergarten geckos this week. We watch them with wonder as they evoke in us a millennia long gone by, and suggest primordial times never seen by human eyes. This morning, an ecstatic "Mom, come here; they're molting!" blasted through the house. I bounded upstairs, dogs hot on my heals, and we all knelt before the aquarium. Right against the glass, a cricket was shedding an old shell, emerging, looking pale and fragile. We watched quietly, with an air of wonder and reverence. We were witnessing a metamorphosis—a crusty, undersized shell left behind, a tentative renewed being stepping forth.

When we allow life to touch us, we molt often, becoming changed, expanded beings. Events that trigger molting often hurt, and the molting itself can be painful. We emerge from outgrown psychic shells awkward, shaky, and vulnerable. Not fully appreciating the process before us, we sometimes try to avoid the pain, losing the opportunity to grow.

Through pain, we further and birth new parts of ourselves. It is pain that nudges us up the steps and urges us to clean out the rooms of our attics, clearing out the recesses of our long overused caches.

We have, in our lives, areas that are particularly painful to us. These issues tend to be thematic throughout our lives. They reoccur and cause us great sorrow. Physical affliction, emotional blockage, and external conditions can leave us feeling frozen and numb. They leave the waters of our lives highly agitated, difficult to navigate. Embracing these issues can transform them into keys to the great doors of internal possibility. They help us manifest our dreams and propel us forward. The benefits that we reap from these openings are exponential. Like traveling through a wormhole or stepping through a secret doorway in a labyrinth, working at these issues cuts days off our arduous journey. Authentically moving through difficult emotional and physical terrain catapults us into realizing our own imaginings.

We would not do this work if we did not have to. We would not decide one splendid morning, "Oh, I think I'll dredge up some old issues." No, it is pain who invites us to the work table and makes it imperative that we find our peace.

We can distract ourselves from the howls of our pain and the rattling of our inner doors with addictions and sidetracking, but when we are still with ourselves, we know. We know that we are not all we are meant to be. We grieve. The nymph of our full potential haunts us with her songs, provoking us into authenticity. We yearn, on a visceral level, to be fully alive—to be full potential beings. It is only through repeated firing that clay turns into the beautiful vases we admire. Firing at heats in excess of 2000° creates the exotic and provocative patterns of Raku. And so it is with us. Through firing, we become more than we were; we transform. We are wedged and pulled, shaped and reshaped, fired, glazed, and refired into sublime forms.

One of our roles as we walk through the fires in our lives is one of midwife. The pain and the angst are opportunities for new life. A midwife cannot stop labor pains, but she can lighten our burden through her compassionate support. She has witnessed many births, and she is an archetype of new beginnings. She knows and trusts the process. She respects the pain. Her gentle, sound presence grounds us.

Life can feel viciously cruel and heartless at times as many attempts are miscarried and tossed aside. Our job as midwife is to stay focused on the forest and not be distracted by the roar of a falling tree. The process is grand. Expansion and growth are wondrous, and birth is miraculous. Being a midwife requires us to be anchored in, and trusting of, the creative force of the universe. This archetypal birthing resounds deeply within us. We know this process on a visceral level. We need to trust in it and turn ourselves over to the deeper, more primal levels of our psyche so that we may be swept along on the contractions that emanate from this place.

Perspective is crucial, for it soothes our achings and quiets our fears. As we move through difficult landscapes, our raconteur needs to speak to us of mythic journeys, reminding us that our pain is needed to bring forth new life. Perspective allows us to use our pain. It allows us to join the process rather than fight it.

Fear and constriction make labor harder. Unlike physical births, we can affect the end result of emotional labors. We can push an emerging self back down and prolong the labor process indefinitely. We can even refuse to birth at all. If we do, we will be spared the immediate agony of labor, but we will reap chronic lethargy and sorrow at the loss of possibility. Life will seem "less than."

It is a tricky thing to aid the birthing process while giving birth. But we have the ability to pass back and forth between roles. We can drop our outer selves and plunge deep inside, trusting where we are carried. When we stay connected to the greater story of our lives we can see the forest from the trees. The darker passes that pain create can be walked with dignity, if not ease. The challenging times in life are riddled with bounty. Surrendering ourselves to the process, not fighting every step of the way, we leave our hands free to scoop up the diamonds these difficult trails reveal.

$$\left(\!8\!\right)$$

Nice to Meet You
The Relationship that Centers It All

OUR RELATIONSHIP WITH OURSELVES DETERMINES the internal highways upon which we travel. Will we midwife ourselves from the high road of our authentic self, with all its ensuing creativity and power? Or, will we midwife ourselves from the lower roads of our false selves that spiral downward with negativity, with no promise of blossom or fruition? Will we labor for naught?

Our choice affects what kind of access we have to that cosmic ocean of creativity. It determines whether we come to the shore with a dixie cup, or arrive laden with the biggest container we can find, ready to scoop up all the ocean has to offer.

As children, when we are respected for who we are and allowed to be true to ourselves, we naturally develop our authentic selves. Our authenticity keeps us connected to the energy of the universe. Authenticity is a conduit to our higher selves. Honesty opens the doors to higher realms of awareness. It frees us from the minutia of our egos and allows our energy to flow, unblocked, into our true purpose.

We did not choose our parents, at least not on a conscious, present day level. Our souls, perhaps, chose specific experiences for us to further our learning in certain areas. In adulthood, however, we do chose what kind of internal family we live in, and we can be intentional about that choice. Even in choosing not to change our childhood legacies, we make a choice.

How we talk to ourselves, how we think about ourselves and how we feel about ourselves has a tremendous impact on our lives. Our internal landscape determines how we treat ourselves. It determines how we filter comments and interactions with friends, lovers and colleagues. With far reaching implications, our relationship with ourselves is the gatekeeper for our external world, and the mood setter for our internal world. We need to find a style of relating to ourselves that brings out the very best in us and enables us to fully blossom. The right amount of emotional sunshine and rain, the ideal psychic soil with its essential nutrients, allows our beings to bloom, thrive, and fruit bountifully.

Just as children glow in families that are respectful and loving, in families where the communication is open—so do we, as adults, thrive in similar "internal families." Approaching ourselves with respect and love, from a place of openness and non-attack, we become who we hope to be.

In a culture so focused on appearances, it is sometimes convenient for us to slip into seeing ourselves as our behaviors or our external façades. Let's not judge ourselves by our covers, for we are all works in progress. We are not our behaviors, or the personas our egos so often put forth. There is an essence—a godlike substance, if you will—in all of us that is the purest form of who we are. It illuminates us from within, igniting us and those around us with compassion and love. When we clear away the beliefs, attitudes and behaviors that obstruct this radiance, we positively glow. We are boundlessly generous of heart; we become the brilliant beings we are intended to be.

By letting ourselves be drawn to this powerful, magnificent light—by seeking it out, and recognizing it in ourselves and others, even in times of great darkness—we rekindle our authentic beings. Looking beyond the wounded and flawed parts of ourselves, focusing on the light we know to be present at our very center, we align ourselves with our highest beings. Love, unconditionally given, heals our wounds and returns us to our authenticity. All of our harmful behaviors and attitudes can change. They are most likely to change, and in fact will do so, when we are loved, respected and genuinely cared for.

Psychic paralysis overcomes us when we label and limit the views we have of ourselves. The visible, tangible parts of ourselves are such minute pieces of the whole. The judgments, positive or negative, constrict us and make it impossible for us to shine from our true source. Our creativity is blocked. We need our freedom. By determining the kinds of relationships we have with ourselves and others, our thoughts can imprison or set us free.

Like working for a difficult employer, one who treats us with great negativity, when our interactions with ourselves are contrary and disapproving, even the simplest of life's tasks feels arduous. Any delight we might find is squelched by our callous and harsh opinions of ourselves. If we make a mistake, we are left feeling flattened and embarrassed. We are not épanouit; we cannot thrive or bloom in such a setting. On the other hand, when we approach ourselves respectfully and without judgment, solidly anchored in our core, we are able to see beyond the façades of our external selves to our full potential. Beneath a gaze of warmth, we develop into the human beings we dream of becoming. We delve into our existence with excitement and fervor, unlocking our true creative genius.

Unaware of how we treat ourselves, some of us remain embroiled in defeating relationships with ourselves. We have taken over where childhood caretakers left off, not realizing the rut our unconscious habits have driven us into. We vehemently defend our negative relationships, telling ourselves, "I'll change how I talk to myself when I'm more successful," or "When I lose weight, I'll be more gentle with myself," or "When I get higher grades, I'll treat myself better." Tragically, that time never comes, for when we do achieve our desired goals, the bar just moves higher, the carrot inches forward just out of reach, and we have a new reason not to love ourselves fully.

Not caring for ourselves can never be justified, and there is not a soul on the planet who is not deserving of love. Love needs to be given freely and unconditionally. When we dole it out to ourselves in conditional thimblefulls, its potency is severely diluted. We are not perfect, and we are not meant to be. If we were flawless, we would not have incarnated on this planet. Some of us— like Hindi gurus and Christian saints and other sundry people peppered here and there across the globe—are highly evolved beings. But none of us is complete. We are all learning to become whole, returning to the light at our center.

Often coming to us in cryptic casings, mistakes—life's lessons—deserve to be welcomed and used for all they are worth. If we are to crawl through thorns, tearing and ripping our way through brambles, we might as well strive to gather something precious in the process.

Rather than approaching life as a learning process, welcoming challenges, and gleaning new knowledge from our errors, many of us have learned to evaluate ourselves, constantly passing judgment on our worth and demeaning ourselves, thereby dampening our innate impulse toward growth. We have learned to shy away from the risks that would open the gates to our dreams. From this vantage point, life becomes a series of debasing and belittling experiences. We compare ourselves to those around us and expect tremendous performance from ourselves. We zero in on the negatives and miss the positive. Where we might be prone to see the glass as half full, we judge ourselves as being half empty. We become short tempered and unkind in our treatment of ourselves. We attempt to tease greater self performance through conditional affection and judgment.

Some of us have gotten to a place in our lives where we have allowed ourselves to believe that we are not good enough, that life is too hard, and it is just not worth trying anymore. We have bought into the false notion that we are what we do. We equate our behavior with our identity and self worth. Our advertising industry supports us whole heartily in this endeavor, reinforcing that if we drive such and such a car, we are successful; if we wear such and such an after shave, we are sexy; if we are disorganized, we are sloppy; and if we are overweight, we are lazy. These attributes do not mean anything more than what they are—states that are true at a particular moment in time. They tell us nothing about our intrinsic worth.

When we detach from the labels and value judgments thrown at us from within and without, we regain our freedom—we reopen the field, becoming free to trip and fall in this business we call life. When we ignore such judgments, we are free to learn and grow, to try new things, to expand and become more than we were yesterday.

Attacking ourselves takes us further away from our source. To thrive, we need a safe environment and gentle guidance. With internal support, we can live—live fully and richly, boldly pulling our chair up to the banquet of life, helping ourselves to great servings of self-actualization, peace, energy, and joy.

When we shift our attitude to one of support and love, we do not have to constantly defend ourselves, and an abundance of energy becomes available to us. It is exhausting to perpetually be on the defensive, especially when the attack is from within. There is nothing to attack. We simply get misguided and lost at times. Acting from our egos, we make poor choices. The essence within us, however, remains unchanging and eternal, and our value is inherent. We yearn to glow from our core and share our natural brilliance, and we have but to create the climate to make it so.

Our external lives mirror our internal condition. What we see in the world, both positive and negative, is a reflection of our own selves. Our strong, visceral reactions tell us more about ourselves than the outside event or person we are reacting to. They alert us to a rousing of our own internal issues.

For instance, a colleague refusing to help out on a project does not realistically warrant the wave of rage that may sweep across us. Our instinctive reaction warns us of blocked, unprocessed material. We tend to get caught up in the situation, feeling offended by the incident, rather than focusing on the reflection life's mirror is holding up for us. We certainly may need to deal with the person or quandary that has vexed us, but the real pot of gold lies within.

When we find ourselves in difficult situations, whether they are self-created or externally induced, learning from them bestows us with the silver linings these dark clouds conceal. By taking time away from the situation to open ourselves up to the issue, we can silently ask the universe, "What am I meant to learn from this?" Putting the question out, letting it go and accepting the response—whenever and however it comes to us—can lead to amazing results. We may have an immediate epiphany, or the clarity may come several weeks later when we stumble across a book, receive a phone call from an old friend, or hear a song that stirs old memories. Remaining open allows the voyages of our lives to unfold in astonishing ways.

Throughout these travels, our internal dialogue sets the tone for the relationship we have with ourselves. Language is powerful, and how we wield it has a profound influence on our sense of well-being and happiness. Constantly communicating with ourselves and interpreting incoming data, we talk to ourselves all the time. Our narrators ingeniously paint the backdrops of our lives, one colorful word at a time.

Internalizing the communication style of our caretakers, we learn our self-talk in childhood. Our family's style of relating—unless we have changed it as adults—is familiar, and we accept it without contest, sometimes without awareness.

Whether it is flagrant or subtle, some of us not even realizing we are talking to ourselves, our internal repartée has a strong impact on how we feel and the kinds of lives we create. Instantly looping back, we feel the effects of our internal commentary as it is assimilated without struggle. When we receive unwelcome comments from the outside world, our internal censor automatically offers a counter remark that gets processed along with the affront. But when a thought slips in on our self-talk circuit it passes unhindered, without reflection, to the deep recesses of our beings, where it impacts our reality.

Intentionally listening, hearing the words and tones we are using with ourselves, and filtering them against external frameworks we feel comfortable with gives us tools for evaluating our self-talk. How would our internal conversation sound between mother and daughter, father and son, employer and employee, friend and friend? If we find that we are creating a less than encouraging inner ambience, we can interrupt our dialogues and suffuse them with more supportive styles of interaction.

We are trying to remove dust from our lenses, not wage a full blown battle against ourselves, so easy does it. Grinding dirt on glass only scratches it. The point is not to damage ourselves in the process of healing, merely trading one issue for another, leaving us no closer to the light at our center than we were before. When we hear our minds blurting negative, self-abasing comments, we can catch the thoughts and redirect them. Gently countering with, "No, we're not going to talk like that anymore in our family" enables us to stop the negative labeling and block the traffic, keeping it from merrily traveling along usual routes. Impeding the ordinary progression of our interior discourse opens up new possibilities.

Haltingly—perhaps at first—a new style of self-talk will evolve. Trying out others' words and styles of relating may feel awkward and ingenuine, but in time, we will grow into a supportive and dynamic style of our own.

Working our thoughts out with pencil and paper can have a powerful braking effect on runaway negative thinking as well. Actually writing the negative thoughts or beliefs, crossing them out, and replacing them with something like, "We're not going to talk like that anymore; this isn't working" gives us concrete access to elusive thought patterns.

We may need to catch our contrary ways a number of times, for old habits sometimes die hard. But with attention and a willingness to ask for help from our higher source, our harmful self-talk will shift and redirect. The timbre of our communication with ourselves will be forever altered, and we will reap the exponential benefits of a kinder self-relationship, one in which our highest potential is able to unfold and evolve.

We yearn to be self-actualized and live in an environment where we feel free. In righting our relationships with ourselves, we are not inventing some far off new trend, but rather, we are returning home, moving back to the climate in which we thrive—one of love and acceptance.

As we say no to old patterns, we can anticipate initial resistance. Doubtful thoughts will counter our efforts with reasons why we should continue to treat ourselves badly. We can expect such reactions and even welcome them, as they are sure signs that the guard is changing, that the internal order is reshuffling for the better. Changing any homeostasis leads to an initial backlash as old patterns tenaciously try to maintain their status quo.

In the period of time between old and new ways, shadows from the past seem to haunt us. It is as if our minds want to make completely certain that we are dedicated to this new style of relationship before they commit themselves whole heartily. They present us with old thought patterns and phrases, as if to say, "Are you sure you don't want these anymore?" As we change, old issues will resurface, or surface for the first time. Processing them—on our own, with friends, or a therapist—will clear the space for new dynamics of relating. Forging new possibilities in our relationships with ourselves calls for gentle

persistence and patience. If we insist on talking to ourselves more positively, we will, and we will reap the
incredible benefits of a much enhanced sense of well-
being.

A descriptive comment such as "That did not go the
way I wanted it to" is not harmful. It keeps us tuned into
our feelings. When we bash ourselves, we deprive ourselves of the opportunity to process our emotions.
Finding ways to talk to ourselves that are not accusatory,
attacking or labeling of who we are will free us up.

Detachment is critical. Leaving our luggage behind,
solidly rooting ourselves in the moment, and being able
to see clearly without attacking enables us to rearrange
internal landscapes. A disorganized desk is just that—
nothing more, nothing less. It does not mean anything
about our inherent worth as a human being, nor is it a
measure of our value. Just as being the CEO of a multi-
million dollar empire does not mean anything about us
other than the fact that we are the CEO of a multi-mil-
lion dollar empire. We are all lit within from the same
radiant source.

Vibrant life springs from a nourishing self-relationship.
A vital relationship with ourselves allows us to correct
any discordant beliefs; clear out harmful vestiges buried
in the caches of our psyches; and approach life's
inevitable challenges with a sense of trust—trust in ourselves and trust in the universe. A great internal family
launches us and leaves us living in the authentic, in the
possible. When we create and maintain a considerate and
positive relationship with ourselves, the sky is the limit.
We can balloon to the moon—anything is possible.

⑨

Growing into Ourselves
Transforming with Attitude

THERE ARE TIMES WHEN TRANSFORMATION TAKES PLACE on an unconscious level, when we know that something is shifting, but we are not directly encouraging it. We are managing the anxiety and discomfort that comes with such change, but we are not willing it on a conscious level. At other times, we have grown, come upon new insights that make certain of our behaviors or thought patterns no longer acceptable to us and so we intentionally work on changing.

Change is not something that we can force. In fact, there is a strange relationship between acceptance and change. We are in the seemingly odd position of needing to accept the very things we want to change. When we force change, the end result is not real and lasting. We can wrest a surface shift, but the root of the issue will remain and simply manifest elsewhere. Genuine change, root transformation, is not summoned, it is invited into our lives. By opening ourselves to the universe's imprint, by allowing its energy to course through our beings, the universe works through us. It is the creative energy of the cosmos that truly brings about change. When we plant seeds and tend the soil, the force that sparks the metamorphosis of those seeds into plants comes from the universe; it is of us, but not us.

We are predisposed to grow, swelling to our fullest potential. When the internal and external conditions are right, we thrive, instinctively running toward self-actualization. It is only our selves, our egos, and the negative conditioning and lessons that we have learned in life that get in our way. This vital impetus is so apparent in children before they begin to lose contact with their authentic selves. Children want to grow and learn. Passionately reaching for the experiences that move them, voraciously curious and inquisitive, they expand and shrink, remaking themselves on a daily, hourly basis. They are open and fluid in life's hands, willingly turning themselves over to the creative energy that permeates our universe.

Somewhere inside our adult selves, that same pulsating self—with it's strong, natural tendencies toward health, vitality and radiance—yearns to be set free. We have but to create the outward conditions to rejoin our natural flow.

Change requires an environment of acceptance, love and tremendous gentleness. For most of us, the bulk of the work is in the preparation—in the transformation of our self-talk, in finding a way to unconditionally love ourselves.

Perceiving change as a static goal, we sometimes get stuck thinking that we need to be fixed, that we have parts that are broken. Change is a process that is meant to last a lifetime. Hopefully, we are constantly refining and expanding ourselves, aligning ourselves with our higher selves until the two are indistinguishable. This is not a finite process with a set beginning and end, but rather an ongoing process that is constantly shifting. We need to let go of our static, linear thinking.

How often have we started to work on changing something only to think that the results should be noticeable, measurable and fast? We force issues and try to orchestrate the process, creating unnecessary pressure and stress. We inadvertently solidify the very things we are trying to change. Like a Chinese finger puzzle, our urgency anchors our issues more deeply. The more we try to pull our fingers out, the tighter the hold becomes. Only by releasing our grip and moving our fingers deeper into the puzzle, in the seemingly "wrong" direction, will the puzzle release our fingers. Similarly, only by releasing our grip on "negative" habits and attitudes will they be free to transform.

When we feel urgently about changing a certain behavior, we put intense pressure on ourselves. Unfortunately for us, the more pressure we put on ourselves, the more solidly we embed the very trait we want to alter. The more we hate the behavior we want to change, the more we cement it into ourselves. We become impatient, treating ourselves harshly, focusing on the negative. We get into a vicious struggle, pushing even harder out of frustration, resenting the very things we do to work on the issue, locking ourselves into a dangerous and ultimately destructive state of mind, where genuine change cannot possibly take root. It is very much like pounding the soil of our gardens so solidly that a seed could not pierce through and grow, even if it wanted to.

Our task is to open ourselves, taking our cues from the universe. We need to focus on the positives and avoid the quicksand of the negatives. If we truly want peace, we need to love peace, not hate war. The thoughts we focus on manifest.

Doing what we love and loving what we do creates an atmosphere in which our happiness flourishes. What we do does not matter, but how we do it, how we feel about doing it is crucial, as it creates our reality one moment at a time. We need to find ways to love our lives, even if we start with the tiniest portion of it. We will get further by focusing on the one percent that is working for us than by focusing on the ninety nine percent that is not. Loving ourselves, even if we start with an infinitesimal corner of ourselves, propels us towards the changes we desire— and ultimately, happiness—faster than focusing on the parts we dislike and find fault with.

The most productive and authentic transformations come from accepting who and where we are in the moment, and loving ourselves anyway. We can look at ourselves honestly, acknowledging the aspects we want to modify, thinking very gently "Yes, this is how I am acting right now. I don't think this is fantastic, but I can accept it in this moment. It's something that can change. It's not my core being; it's more like the sleeve on my overcoat."

Ultimately, we are not creating change, but rather inviting the universe to bring an energy within us to the forefront and shift another to a more dormant status. When we force issues, we operate from our egos, our small glasses of ocean water, rather than reconnecting with the ocean and operating from our higher selves. Our time is better spent creating internal climates that are receptive to the universe, rather than pushing up streams we can not navigate. We can focus on who we want to become, rather than bemoaning who we are not. We can talk to ourselves with respect and love, opening ourselves to that universal energy that is life-changing.

Love channels creative energy. It is the great pipeline from ourselves to all that is. By creating a supportive environment; fostering a supportive internal family; and remaining grounded in love, no matter what, we can catapult our dreams into realities.

I recently worked with a client who had a tremendous amount of anxiety. He had been highly anxious for a lifetime, and he had become frustrated and tyrannical with his fear. His attitude toward his anxiety served only to cement it more solidly in his life. His bitterness, like concrete, made it impossible for new life to take root. Observing his anxiety, listening to it rather than bulldozing it, he worked on ending the lifelong war he had waged against it. He learned how to write from his anxiety, allowing it to express itself directly, simply accepting it as it was. Gradually, he relaxed and opened up, allowing a different kind of energy into his life. It loosened the soil of his personae, and the seeds of different affects began to sprout. In time, they grew vigorously. He learned to focus on how he wanted to feel, rather than on his anxiety. Shifting from hate to love, he found moments when he was not feeling anxious, and celebrated them grandly. When he felt anxious, he simply noted it. He was not at war with himself anymore, and did not have to fight to make the changes happen. Stuck in his rage, he had been pulling his fingers apart in a Chinese finger puzzle. Accepting his anxiety and curtailing the heartless, demeaning judgments of himself, he moved his fingers together and the "puzzle," his anxiety, released its grip. No longer having to control things he had no power over, he relaxed and opened himself up, trusting the energy around him, trusting that it would shift his anxiety if he did his part. Gradually, my client's anxiety lessened. As it subsided, issues arose that needed to be processed. The original fury over his loss of control had fossilized these issues; his anxiety had frozen them in place. As his anxiety's hold on him receded, issues thawed, came back to life, and my client was able to clear them out. The emotional space he created by accepting his condition, by ending his relentless battle with himself invited change into his life.

The relationship we have with ourselves sets the tone for the voyage. When we have a gentle and loving self-relationship, we do better in all aspects of our lives. Creating the most awesome relationship we can with ourselves lets everything else fall into place.

We need to be able to step back when we deal with ourselves, particularly in times of transformation. We need to give ourselves room. The more we attach to a behavior, in a positive or negative way, the more we cement it into our lives. We do not need to attack a particular behavior or go after it in order to effect a change in our lives. Instead we can simply observe ourselves, watching without judgment. When we slip out of the role of detached observer, we skid onto treacherous territory, fueling the very behaviors we want to let go of. Even when we are thinking about how much we do not want to act or think in a certain way, we are energizing the traits we want to extinguish. When we are being overly critical of ourselves or another, when we allow ourselves to get swept away in the impulse to criticize, we magnify and intensify the negative. When we jump into a vehement self-bashing session we cement the critical aspects of ourselves more solidly in our beings. If we can simply observe the part of us that is being critical, we can stay detached from it, not fueling or energizing it, but giving it room to shift naturally. What we focus on grows.

Behaviors that we deem as not being in our best interest are never about the behaviors themselves. There is always another, less obvious layer. Authentic change needs process on this deeper level; it needs to spring from inside. It requires an observing, caring and gentle self-facilitator; it requires that we not be overly invested in the outcome.

An attitude of acceptance and detachment from the outcome may be difficult for most of us to achieve. We may be able to hold it for some time, only to have it slip again. We have learned that we are what we do, how we act, and how we look. Our core is none of these things. Our egos are overly invested in our actions and activities, and in the labels we and others assign to ourselves.

Locking into a struggle over changing a particular behavior engenders palpable negative energy. We may have the best of intentions, and we may get rid of the behavior out of sheer force, but it will not be lasting and true change. It will not be from the inside out. Therefore, the issues that caused the behavior in the first place will simply manifest elsewhere.

We are not our behaviors, thoughts, or actions. These are subject to radical change throughout our lifetimes. They are but momentary states, blips on the screen of infinity. Our selves, and the many incarnations of those selves that we become in a lifetime, are means to an end. They are simply our modes of transportation, the cars we travel in. They make it possible for us to exist on this physical plane. They are our receivers, the mechanisms by which we take in and filter life. And they are capable of drastically altering at any moment; they are not static facts.

Being wary of our labeling and judgmental tendencies, we need to be willing to approach life from a clean slate, one of acceptance. When we detach from the outcome, when we stay in the moment it is easier, in fact effortless, to be patient, accepting and loving with ourselves and others. We cannot push the river. In changing ourselves, we are trying to bring out the best, we are not trying to get rid of anything. Certain qualities are moving to the foreground, while others are fading into the background.

We originally developed our "negative" tendencies and

habits to take care of ourselves. They are nothing more than protective coatings, coping mechanisms. And while some of these overcoats would now serve us better retired to an attic closet, we need to remember that they once served a purpose. They shielded us from fear, and our feelings of vulnerability.

We are doing the best we can in each moment. If we are engaged in harmful behaviors, it is because we do not have a sense of alternate and valid choices. We may be unconsciously scared away by the emotional material hidden behind the behaviors. Even when we are doing something that is hurting us—like overeating, drinking, or smoking—on some level, we are trying to take care of ourselves. We have gotten hooked into thinking that these things will help us feel better. We are trying to change, our core always striving for clarity and authenticity. We are doing the best we can.

Approach is everything. Genuine change flows out of acceptance and love. We do not have to love all of our behaviors or attitudes, but we do need to accept them without judgment and love ourselves in spite of them. We need to remember that our core, the essence of who we are, is pure light. We all have behaviors that are in need of modification, but this does not affect our worth or the indisputable fact that we are deserving of love.

We cannot grow in a pool of internal negativity and pressure. It is impossible. What appears to be change is not true and valid. It is a shifting of issues, pushing one down only to have another pop up somewhere else. Like filling a mole hole in our yard and thinking "This is wonderful; I've gotten rid of the mole," well, no, the mole has just made three more holes somewhere else on the lawn. This has not solved anything, just displaced it. And in fact, it has actually made matters worse.

Transformation takes time. Everything does not always happen as quickly as we think it should. The most exquisite landscapes on our planet were formed over huge periods of time. Transforming, evolving ourselves into our most splendid possible beings and sharing that splendor is our true purpose. Certainly we can accord this work a lifetime. A lifetime of tending to the possibilities, plowing dreams into realities, and sowing love—whenever and wherever we can—is indeed well spent.

To Me With Love
The Art of Journaling

JOURNALING, CHRONICLING OUR STORIES TO OURSELVES, opens doors to multiple possibilities. When we are lost in an internal fog of emotion, we can work ourselves back to a place where we have perspective one word at a time. Frequent journaling allows us to maintain a relationship with ourselves. If we are to act as effective and dynamic midwives, we need to be engaged in an ongoing and open dialogue with ourselves. Our relationship needs to be honest, the paths of communication clear and accessible. If we have not been communicating with ourselves, if our communication has been negative or callous, it will take time for those injuries to heal. But heal they will if we stay committed.

Commitment, openness, and caring detachment heal. Like a parent with an angry teenager, it takes time to bridge the gap of a torn relationship. A parent cannot simply announce "We're going to have a great relationship now" and expect it to be so. No, this parent has to be willing to show up, trusting that this relationship can heal, trusting in something beyond him or herself. When the first "Sarah would you like to have breakfast with me?" is greeted with harumps and groans, this parent might just offer "Well, I'm going to be here every morning, and I would love it if you'd join me." Then that parent needs to let it go, doing his or her part by showing up at the breakfast table with a heart open to the possibilities. After many days, and many groans, moans and slammed doors later, one morning this teenager might just plop herself into a kitchen chair, mumbling something about the food at school being terrible, so she might as well have a piece of toast at home. Eventually, if this parent continues to show up at the breakfast table with an open, caring detachment, this adolescent will tentatively reach out and eventually reconnect. This child wants the connection.

We want the connection with ourselves. In fact, we need this connection if we are to thrive. And when we regularly show up at our own breakfast tables, inviting and making room for all the parts of ourselves, our own disenfranchised parts, with their inherent energy, join us as well.

Journaling is like showing up at the breakfast table. Through our journaling, we give voice to the internal chatter; we vent it. When we turn ourselves over to our writing, it becomes cathartic. Catharsis—from the Greek word katharsis, meaning to purge, to purify—makes space.

We can use our writing to express our feelings, to sort

out our thoughts, or to let opposing views joust and spar it out. Turning the pen over to our unconscious, we can let the words flow. Stepping back and allowing ourselves to write from a practically unconscious stance can be a revealing experience. Documenting what comes to mind without processing it, taking dictation from the deeper realms of our beings and only later going back to read what we have written, can bring us guidance and a different framework for issues we feel stumped by. We can even initiate such journaling with a particular question, letting ourselves relax deeply, and writing what comes to us.

We can be intentional about our writing, we can become more conscious of our self-talk as we write it out; we can help ourselves get back on track if need be. We cannot reconnect with our higher selves if we have gotten sidetracked by ego. Supporting ourselves as we would support a loved one, we can salve our wounds and bring ourselves back onto our paths.

Our bodies often express what we dare not give voice to directly. We can turn pen and paper over to our aches and pains. What would the searing pain in our lower back say if it had words? What would the tension in our shoulders say if it could talk? We can let the words float out from deep within us onto the paper, trying to keep our objective, thinking mind out of the way.

Setting aside a period of time every day to write keeps us focused. The many activities in our twenty-first century schedules vie for our time, and establishing a daily ritual around journaling will ensure that we get at least a minimum of writing in every day. It is our time to tune in to ourselves and listen to what is really going on inside us. What are we saying to ourselves? What screenplays are we producing? What beliefs are we supporting?

Carrying a small journal with us makes it more likely that we will write at other times throughout the day as well. In time, we will naturally turn to this wonderfully soothing activity during times of stress and confusion, finding clarity through our writing.

The benefits that we reap over time from maintaining a correspondence with ourselves are many. The journaling process turns on another modality; it expands our thinking. It gets stuck trains moving.

Dropping Down the Well

Reconnecting With Our Intuition

WE HAVE INTERNAL ACCESS TO ABSOLUTELY EVERY SINGLE piece of wisdom we will ever need. Partnering with our higher selves takes our lives from an outdated black and white television screen to a full color, surround sound, technicolor movie screen. It takes us to new levels, inviting the infinite back into our lives and welcoming our soul's deep wisdom to our tables. Enhancing our psychic vision gives life profound meaning, broadening the vistas we are capable of taking in. Sharing the burden for our daily lives, taking our cues from the universal wisdom within us, smoothes the rocky roads and precipitous cliffs we will sometimes find ourselves struggling to cross.

Our relationship with our higher selves, and thus to

infinite creativity, is one we need to cultivate. Taking our small glass of ocean water, we pour ourselves back into that powerful body of water, reconnecting with the tremendous energy we are a part of. We reap phenomenal benefits from this return to our source. Our soul resonates with the frequency of the infinite, with all that is, and when we are plugged in to our core, everything feels as it should. We feel expanded and energized. Puzzles make sense as we watch the pieces fall into place.

Our daily struggles can be turned over to this place, to our higher selves. So much of our strife has answers waiting in the wings if we will merely take the time to ask the questions, and be still and patient enough to wait for the answers. The voice of our higher selves, of our intuition, whispers. It is quieter than the prattle of our daily lives, and we need to make room for its presence by creating solitude, stillness, and quiet. Making space in our psyches, leaving our egos at the door, we cultivate our relationships with our higher selves, reopening our conduits to the wisdom which lives in all of us just below the surface. This wisdom is soothing and grounding, as well as energizing. It is always available to us. But, like a radio frequency, we need to tune in to it.

Tuning in to this perhaps unfamiliar frequency may be frustrating at first. We may not be able to readily connect with our intuition. Stilling our minds enough to hear the whispers of our intuition may prove challenging. Like cutting through very dense foliage in a forest for the first time, we may feel that our progress is negligible. Initially, we may not be able to find our way in the thick underbrush. If we continue to return day after day, however, a path will open up to us. With much travel, the road will become well-worn and easily discernible. We will have access to these intuitive byways throughout our day. We will be able to access the great wisdom of our intuition simply by bringing it into our awareness.

Meditation is one of the more common ways of accessing our higher wisdom. Meditation takes many forms, and we need to find a way that works for us. We need to quiet our outer selves, our egos, so that we can hear the whispers of our inner selves. Physical activities, such as running, swimming, and horseback riding can still our minds by quieting the incessant internal dialogue. Giving ourselves permission to get lost in a game of tennis can sidetrack us out of the overdrive of our daily lives. A mindful walk through nature, yoga, and Tai Chi soothes our ruffled feathers. These practices help us center ourselves, directing our attention inward. Breathing, controlled and purposeful deep breathing, is also a great shortcut to serenity. How often we may find ourselves taking hurried, shallow breaths as we rush through our days. Stopping for a few minutes and breathing deeply can bring clarity to an out-of-focus world. And this is something we can do anywhere, anytime.

Keeping an awareness of this inner realm throughout each day forms a bridge from our physically grounded outer world to our intuitively grounded inner world thus allowing us access to the full range of our psyches. Remembering that there are deeper planes to our existence than the obvious, material ones keeps us connected to them and allows us access to the knowledge and peace that lie therein. Accepting that everything is exactly as it is meant to be in this moment allows us to turn inward for guidance. It frees us from the extreme stress of trying to orchestrate the details of our lives. It allows copilots into our cabin.

We do not have to do this all by ourselves. In fact, our higher self—our higher power, or whatever we choose to call this energy—is always ten steps ahead of us. We do not have to figure it all out. Our job is to follow the cues our higher selves have laid out for us. We are at our optimal, in all walks of life, when we operate from our higher selves. There is nothing we can do better from the position of our egos.

We are spiritual and physical beings, of both worlds. When we straddle our inner and outer realties, our feet are solidly planted in both realms. We thrive—mind, body, and soul—as we hold our total grandness with its infinite vistas of possibility. A daily practice that releases stress, quiets our minds and bodies, and increases our awareness of our connection to our inner guidance keeps us well-balanced on the high wire of life.

Gremlins
The Critters We Live With

A LESS THAN SAVORY CAST OF CHARACTERS—our gremlins, the henchmen and women of our egos—resides in all of us, somewhere in the shadows of our beings. We can tell when our gremlins are at the helm of our lives because we feel miserable in an insidious kind of way. Executing our ego's every order, they keep us off balance, out of kilter, hesitant and awkward as we move through our lives.

Megaphone in hand, this cast of characters sits tall on our shoulders, spewing a series of "not so helpful" running commentaries. They are the experts on our every mistake and dare not miss an opportunity to point out where we have gone wrong. They are the kings and queens of the sarcastic, cutting comment: "Mmm, couldn't you have done that better?" "Oh, you really messed that one up, that figures!" "You're not really going to do that, are you?" "You don't deserve something that nice."

With their cryptic little jabs leading the way, these

gremlins surreptitiously invade our lives. Before we know it, we have handed over a loud speaker and a director's chair, putting them in charge of our lives. Each of these gremlins travels with an entourage of actors, set designs, scripts and props. They create incredibly realistic portrayals of life as a dreary, depressing pastime in which we could never hope to find fulfillment or joy. It is quite possible to find ourselves so completely caught up in the realism of the show that we forget that this is a show. We lose the thread of our life stories. We sidestep into an alternate reality, and the mirage is complete because as we cross over into this parallel life, we lose any memory of our "real" life.

Gremlin Theater productions are unsurpassed for their artful delivery, their extreme realism, and their ability to engage the audience. They are guaranteed to leave us flattened and despondent. Some of the more renowned gremlins from this grand troupe of performers include the Critic, the Blamer, Sir Comparison and Mademoiselle Envy. A feisty group of negativity they leave us insecure and ambivalent.

The Critic seems to know how to do everything and has an opinion about everything. In whatever endeavor we care to undertake, he finds us perpetually lacking. The Critic drops pessimistic pilings for us to stumble across. The Blamer, bombastic in her presentation, knows why the world does not work—"It's Henry's fault," "It's the milk industry's fault," "It's the president's fault." She keeps us from ourselves and our own innate power, focusing us ever outward, leaving us peering at others, hoping they will change so that we can feel better.

Sir Comparison is always at the ready, note pad in hand, keeping score. "Oh, that shirt isn't as nice as mine." "Hmm, that car is bigger than mine." "Oh, that's a nicer house." He keeps us seeped in triviality. He convinces us of our differences and leaves us feeling better, or worse, than others, decidedly separate and alone.

Sir Comparison often travels with Mademoiselle Envy—"Oh, I wish I had that," "I'd be so much happier if I had that job," "I'd be so much prettier if I had that hair." She makes sure we know that we are lacking—that we do not have enough money, clothes, energy etc. She keeps us convinced that the key to happiness remains beyond the boundaries of ourselves.

These are but a few of the players in the Gremlin troupe's wide array of character actors. Their depressing effect on our lives is predictable. These actors are superlative at their trade, and we forget that we are participating audience members, present of our own accord.

Gremlinic performances, while riveting and realistic, are predictable and repetitive. Familiar sound bites can tip us off to our unintentional foray into Gremlin Alley. Realizing where we are and what we are listening to can help us back peddle out of this self-defeating theater.

While we have a seemingly endless supply of these gremlins, we each have a cast of two or three that is particularly active. It behooves us to familiarize ourselves with them. We can then personalize and caricaturize them, giving them names. We can humorously wonder "Who let them back into the theater?" as we back away from them.

Attacking these curmudgeons does not work. It

strengthens their foothold and gives their messages validity. Arguing with them tells them they have a point. They do not have a point! Their negativity solely serves our egos—keeping our egos alive and our selves disconnected from our true source.

The kinds of gremlins living in the boarding houses of our psyches may be based on our childhoods and voices from the past, but their raison d'être is to ensure our ego's longevity. They perpetuate our ego's propaganda. Feeding off their frenzied energy, they sing for the joy of hearing their own voices.

Some of the themes purported by our gremlins loop back to our beliefs, infusing them with an extra dose of validity in our own minds, as they are consistent with our internal views of the world and ourselves. A "Poor me, life is lousy" gremlin is fueled by and bolsters an "I don't deserve to be happy; I don't deserve to have a good life" belief. Retiring gremlins needs to happen in conjunction with eliminating self-defeating, harmful beliefs.

Visualizing these gremlinic productions at work and actively shifting what we see is powerful. As we visualize the set and actors, we can imagine our own crew of "good do-bees" coming in and changing the scene. We can watch them carry off the set, clear the props, roll up the backdrop, and slap a big CANCELED DUE TO LACK OF INTEREST notice across the marquee at the front of the theater.

Like everything else in life, an ounce of prevention is worth its weight in gold. It is far easier to catch ourselves as we are lured off by our negative voices than to pull ourselves out of years of residing in their dark passes.

Awareness, commitment and a sense of humor help us maintain an even keel.

⑬

Have We Had Our Laugh Today?
Keeping Ourselves Light

Humor CRACKS THE VENEER OF OUR ROOT-BOUND EGOS and lets bursts of fresh air into our psyches. When we take ourselves too seriously, we pound the soil into a solid mass, making it impossible for new life to sprout. We need to keep our soil loose, tilling it with laughter and comedy, keeping it light.

Being able to laugh at ourselves, and to chuckle at our mistakes, makes learning life's lessons so much easier. It makes us willing to take chances and embrace our lives more completely, enthusiastically meeting the challenges that come our way. Learning to ice skate at seventy-three takes a great sense of humor, and a willingness to laugh heartily when we topple backwards, feet reaching for the heavens. The ability to crack a smile as we hit the same flat note for the seventh time bestows us with the fortitude and patience to attempt it an eighth time. Cheer helps smooth the way in any endeavor, particularly this life mission that engages us all.

When we lose our comic perspective, or when we have not developed it at all, we begin to take our lives very seriously, inviting feelings of self-consciousness, inflated self importance, shame and embarrassment. The stakes, along with our anxiety level, are heightened. Like walking a tight rope with someone pushing from behind, we feel threatened, overwhelmed with inordinate stress and tension. A sense of apprehension and danger lurks in the unknown circumstances of our existences. We become overly cautious, cutting ourselves off from life's experiences in an attempt to control them and protect ourselves. When we give up our laughter, we deprive ourselves of the fastest acting stress reducer we have. Abandoning humor, we constrict ourselves out of our freedom, and it is in freedom that we excel in our authenticity, creating a deep sense of contentment and happiness.

Self-importance, one of our ego's greatest illusions, is completely counter-productive to self-actualization. Laughing at ourselves and enjoying our humanness, short circuits our ego's hold on us. We do not expect perfection when we are chuckling, and our self-consciousness evaporates. When we are giggling, everything feels as it should. Totally present in the moment, past and future drop away, allowing us to function freely. Contagious laughter melts our self-discernment and we are left authentic, if only for a moment or two. We cannot negotiate pretenses and falsities, or entertain limiting beliefs, when we are in the grips of hysterical laughter. There simply is not enough room for anything beyond the guffaws. When we are laughing, really laughing from our hearts, we are open and available. In finding a way to laughter, we find a shortcut to our selves.

Silliness keeps us from taking ourselves too seriously. It is a great elixir for our soul, keeping us light and fluid. It reminds us to remain somewhat unattached to this physical world of ours, taking it all with a grain of salt, thereby leaving us more willing to venture off into other, nonphysical, aspects of our existences.

We are physical and spiritual beings, meant to travel in both spheres. When we become overly grounded in ourselves and the importance of our physical reality, we lose our connection to the ethereal world. Clinging to overly narcissistic and serious views of ourselves, peace and happiness elude us. Melting the shackles our egos all too willingly clap on our psyches, our laughter returns us to an open state where creative energy has room to flow and manifest in endless ways. Creating emotional space, comedy beckons magic and wonder back into our lives.

While there are many sobering complexities and issues in life that are deserving of our attention, our self-importance is not one of them. When we bring ourselves to any task with overly charged egos, we offer far less than we are capable of. The ability to roar, uninhibited, with laughter erects islands where we can rest our weary souls as we swim across treacherous oceans. Healing and renewing us, creating lightness in dark corridors, humor balances us and keeps us on track.

$$(14)$$

That's a Fire
Do We Really Want to Throw Water On It?

THE DAWN OF HUMANKIND FOUND US SCAMPERING and scavenging to survive, at the mercy of external conditions with little opportunity for intentional existence. Fire, and our early ancestor's ability to use it, changed that. We discovered what it felt like to feel warm on frigid mornings, to light up the darkness of the night, and to defend ourselves with a powerful new weapon against sudden attacks by hungry animals. The quality of our prehistoric lives soared.

Fire, this gift from the lightning bolts that struck fiercely at the trees around us, was coveted and guarded. Not knowing how to start fire, we protected it fiercely once nature handed us a burning branch. We traveled for food, hunting and gathering. Protecting our burning coal in a sheath of leather, we discovered how to carry fire with us. Keeping that ember glowing was crucial to our survival as we wandered across the wilderness.

Today, as we trek across the unknown territories of life, keeping the fire at the core of our essence alive is paramount to our survival, sanity and well-being. The flame of our quintessence lights us up from within. While that brilliant fire at our center will never die out, it can become so obstructed and dampened by life and our ego's illusions that we do not get the slightest light or warmth from it.

When our fires are burning brightly, and we have unobstructed access to them, our hearts are open and we are connected to the universe's infinite fields of creativity. We are caring, loving, compassionate and generous. What a world we could create—one impassioned fire at a time!

Tending to the blazes that ignite the darkness with light is a crucial task. How much money we make in our nine-to-five jobs, how many records we break at the state track meet, or how many people voted for us is of no import if we can not feel the fires within our souls. Without that light from within, we are stumbling, blindly in the dark.

Correcting limiting beliefs, clearing out emotional caches, and optimizing our relationship with ourselves creates radiant fires with unhindered access to their brilliance and warmth. We need to know our embers intimately and monitor them with care, noticing what makes them glow brighter, erupting in full flame, and what it is that is happening in our world when they are nearly smothered. Remaining vital in the arctic conditions we sometimes encounter in this life on earth dictates that we remain connected to the heat and glow of our inner presence. Stoking and banking our fires fortifies us for the hard, icy times, and it enables us to enjoy the summer's harvests to the fullest of our potential.

Our greatest accomplishments cannot genuinely sparkle in a somber interior, no matter what the outside world or our egos would have us believe. However, the fire that lights us up from within can illuminate even the bleakest aspects of our lives, delivering a resplendent and heart-warming spectacle. And while our external trophies do not mean a thing in and of themselves—being merely icing on the cake—when we tend to our fires, dreams fall into place, often in ways we never envisioned, even in our wildest dreams.

Our fires glow when we feel alive and vibrant, and roar when we feel ecstatic. We may have to learn how to tolerate the heat, stretching ourselves in new ways, learning that we deserve such incredible energy. The more aware we become of our fires and the more we tend to them, the brighter they burn. The more gratitude we feel for the extraordinary fervor at our center, the more awed we allow ourselves to be by it, the more dazzling it seems to grow.

The journey is a grand one. Keeping our fires burning brightly, and ourselves true, clears the way for the flow of the universe's currents. Even the sky is not the limit. So grab a balloon and reach for the moon.

APPENDIX
The exercises

Exercise 1
THROUGH THE EYES OF INNOCENCE

EVERYTHING WE SEE AS ADULTS, we see through the shades of bias. The innocence and abandon that children meet the world with is a result of the clarity of their vision. There are no judgments because their storehouses of experience are empty. A spoon is a piece of metal with a smooth shape that feels cold when you first pick it up and warms as you hold it. It has no associations with food or kitchens.

This exercise is meant to be done in a spirit of lightness and fun. Select four or five ordinary objects—such as a spoon, a cassette, or a book—and arrange them near you as you begin this exercise. Close your eyes and relax profoundly. Take a few minutes to breathe deeply, breathing out any tension and breathing in relaxation. When you open your eyes, imagine that you are from another planet, and that the things you see around you are foreign and make no sense. Examine the objects you have set out for yourself, work at seeing them with totally receptive, non-judgmental, non-biased eyes—see these trinkets through the eyes of a child.

Once you have become comfortable with this exercise, it can be done spontaneously throughout your day. Practice looking at the world with a renewed and fresh perspective.

Exercise II
RELAXING TO THE CORE

Find a place and some time where you will not be interrupted for at least fifteen minutes. Sit or lie in a comfortable position and allow yourself to relax. Starting with the top of your head, relax your scalp, your eyes, ears, nose and mouth. Relax all the muscles you use to express your personality. Breathing deeply, breathe relaxation into your neck and throat, across your shoulders and upper arms. Pull the calm into your lower arms, wrists and hands. Let any tension flow harmlessly back into the universe through the palms of your hands. Relax your chest and torso, your upper and lower back. Relax your abdomen and your pelvic area. Give your hips and buttocks permission to let go, to rest. Draw the serenity into your thighs, pulling it down into your knees, calves and ankles. Allow your feet a total vacation, letting them know that you do not need them right now.

Continuing to breathe deeply, scan your body for any tension. If you find any stress, breathe light into that area, releasing any tension. Then, imagine yourself drifting on a cloud in a magnificently lit blue sky. You are floating, weightless, at peace with the universe. You feel surrounded by white light. Every molecule in your body is breathing in that healing white light until you are so filled with white light that you are glowing. Allow yourself to stay in this relaxed state for as long as you like. Some people like to do this exercise before bed.

Exercise III
A Few Moments in Time

This exercise is designed to create stillness within. Starting with small increments of time, you can gradually expand your capacity for stillness.

Sit in a comfortable position with your back straight. Relax and set a timer for five minutes. This exercise may be easier to do if it is done after "Relaxing to the core."

There is nothing to do here but simply "be." Notice the thoughts and sensations that come to you, then very gently give them permission to drift away. You can imagine a pond and that you are trying to still the surface. Breathe deeply and gently bring yourself back to the breath when you find you have strayed.

Ideally, this exercise is done daily. At first, five minutes may feel like torture, but in time, this meditation will become easier. When the time feels right, you can increase the amount of time you sit by five minutes, working up to a duration that feels optimal for you.

Do not worry if you cannot still your mind. Returning to this exercise daily you will soon find yourself creating an atmosphere of tranquility.

Using the image of the pond, you can imagine yourself going deeper and deeper down into that pond, like a pebble slowly dropping down, down, down. As you move into the deeper realms of your core, you will feel yourself relaxing more and more completely, relinquishing the thoughts and concerns of your every day life.

BALLOON TO THE MOON ─────────────

Exercise IV
WISDOM'S PLACE

Following a relaxation session, sit in a comfortable position with your back straight and allow yourself to listen to the sound of your deep breathing. With every breath, imagine that you are being drawn deeper and deeper inside, feeling more and more centered and at peace. Allow yourself to be drawn to your place of inner wisdom. You may find yourself on a beach, a mountain top, at the seaside, in a grotto, or in some place you do not recognize as being of this earth. This place feels wonderful, warm and inviting. As you settle in, you feel the powerful energy around you. You feel as if your soul has come home. You may be alone or in the company of another being.

If there are particular issues that you would like to have addressed, you can put them out now. You may get a response right away—an image, a sound, some words—or you may get no response at this time. Either way is great, just accept it as it happens for you, trusting in your own inner wisdom and its timing. Stay in this place until you feel you are done for now, remembering that this is a place that you can come to at any time; this place is you.

As you end this exercise for now and come back to the present, bring with you the sense of relaxation and centeredness, the renewed energy that you feel.

Exercise V
LIFTING THE LID ON BELIEFS

We all have beliefs that we are unaware of that impact our lives powerfully. This exercise is designed to help you discover some of these beliefs and bring them out into the light of day so that you can make some choices about where you would like to go with them.

It is best to do this exercise as you read it, jotting down the first things that come to mind, then later going back and exploring the issues more thoroughly.

Being a woman/man is _____.

People with money are _____.

People who are happy are_____.

Finding fulfillment in life is _____.

Honesty causes _____.

If I truly did what I wanted I'd_____.

The world is _____.

Marriage creates _____.

Getting up for work makes me_____.

Working for a living is _____.

Life should be more_____.

My body is _____.

Physical health comes from _____.

You can spin off on this list, creating new statements to complete in areas of your life that need particular attention. You can also do this with a friend, exploring beliefs and helping each other find the blind spots.

The most important aspect of this exercise is that it be done without thought, using the first words that come to mind.

Exercise VI
TRACKING THE SOURCE

You can do this exercise with any belief you want to explore further. Deconstructing and challenging beliefs are powerful tools in rebuilding a foundation that works in your life. Some of your beliefs are founded on events that are no longer valid.

Select a belief from the previous exercise that you'd like to work on. Write it at the top of the page and add "because..." and complete that sentence. Then complete "Which means..." Finally, answer "Which means what about me?" Take this down the line as far as you can until you feel you've reached the truest and most powerful version of your belief.

Each belief is based on a well of varying depth. The following example, like stepping down a ladder into that well, takes you to the core.

Tracking a belief might look like this:

The world is a terrible place.
Because...
People do awful things.
Which means?
People hurt each other.
Which means what about me?
People will hurt me.
Because...
I can't protect myself.
Which means what about me?

I'm weak.
Which means...
I'm no good.

Behind every belief that is vague and generalized, there is a core belief about ourselves. That's the one we're after; that's the one we're in a position to do something about.

Once you get a core belief, such as "I'm no good," you can make a list of why you think that is so. Then, shift roles and become the objective reporter—gather information that counters each statement on your list; shift your thinking from absolute statements about a certain belief to occasional or time limited statements. There is a tremendous difference between "I'm a procrastinator" and "sometimes, I procrastinate." Even if it feels like I have always procrastinated up to now, the "sometimes I procrastinate" leaves room for change.

When you take on a belief, you unconsciously gather information to support that belief. In this exercise, you're beginning to discredit, or at least cast some serious doubt on, that belief. When you become an "objective reporter" you're telling your brain that you're looking for different kinds of information now. If you continue to chip away at the belief, it will eventually give way to more supportive ones.

Exercise VII
WILL YOU COME OUT AND PLAY?

Take yourself to a store where art supplies are sold, even the local grocery store will do. Find the art section and allow your inner toddler to pick out what he or she would like—such as crayons, paints, color papers, beads and string, or playdough. Buy what you would buy if you were going to put on an awesome play date for a group of four year olds.

Then set yourself up somewhere that you know you will not be disturbed—somewhere you know you will have peace and quiet for a time. Now play! Let yourself enjoy the sensation of what you're doing, not having a care for the product. The product is absolutely irrelevant; the exploration and freedom are the object. Have fun!

Exercise VIII - Part 1
ONCE UPON A TIME

This exercise is designed to help you take a look at the backdrop against which you play out your life. We all have a story; what's yours?

Though we may not consciously think about our stories on a daily basis, they are the internal foundations upon which we create our ongoing experiences. They are the templates for our future.

Write your story out. Write it as a tale, in the third person—"Once upon a time, a little girl was born in a big city. Her mother was scared because etc."

If you like, you can work from a sketchy outline of the major events in your life, but primarily let the story flow as it comes to you. Don't worry about the factual accuracy. You're looking for the overall flavor or feeling of this tale.

When you've written your story, set it aside for at least a week. Then come back and read it. How does this story leave you feeling? What is likely to happen next in this story?

000

Exercise VIII - Part 2
Once upon a new time

What kind of story did the last exercise yield? If it left you feeling hopeless, dulled and dejected, then perhaps a rewrite is in order.

Step back from the story, feel it non personally. This is the story of a hero traversing difficult terrain. There have been many trials. How has this hero grown through the years? What has s/he learned? Whose lives has s/he touched?

As you move through this exercise you will likely need to keep your ego in check, making sure that your ego isn't sabotaging the story at every turn. Don't let yourself be talked into believing that there's no way to rewrite this story or see it differently. That is simply not true. The story is in the perspective, not in the facts. And our perspective launches our future. The view we have today creates the reality we live tomorrow.

Exercise IX
A WEB OF DREAMS

As we move further and further into adulthood we sometimes lose our dreams. Life hurries us along with chores and responsibilities and we forget. In this exercise we'll access old dreams and reactivate the dreamer within. This exercise should be done in the spirit of fun, not pushing or forcing responses. You may have to do this exercise several times before you start getting responses. That's okay. Be patient. If you haven't dreamed in a while it will take a while for your dreamer to know that you're serious about wanting to hear from him or her.

Find a comfortable spot where you won't be interrupted for a while and sit down with some paper and crayons or markers. Start in the middle of the page by drawing a balloon with the word "dreams" in it. Then start webbing out—draw a line to another balloon and in that balloon write down a dream you had as a child. This might be something like: "fly to the moon," "dance," "run a marathon," "be a star," "drive a fire truck," etc.

Let your imagination go. Play, have fun with this exercise. As you move more into present day dreams or new dreams you may start to hear gremlins commenting on the impossibility of such and such a dream. Just acknowledge their presence and carry on.

This is a great exercise to do over time. Come back to it. Play with it. Post it on the wall and add things as you think of them. You might even want to get a poster size sheet of paper and incorporate drawing or a collage. Get as creative as you like. *Have fun.*

Exercise X
AH, THE MUSIC

Music—the provocative medium of the ages—can reach past our barriers, deep into our psyches. Music can set the tone. It can change a mood, alter a perception, rekindle memories. Music has the power to make us weep, laugh or sleep.

You can consciously use music in a great variety of ways. You can listen and dance to music as a way to revitalize yourself, or shift a lethargic mood. You can play a piece of music that reminds you of a loved one who has died, in order to shed a backlog of tears that have accumulated within. You can follow through on hunches for music—if you feel drawn to a certain song or piece of music, play it, trust your intuition. It may be reaching past your consciousness releasing its healing properties deep within.

Give yourself permission to experiment with music. Take some time and play different pieces of music. Watch yourself react to them.

Make a list—"for a rainy day"—of music that is soothing and uplifting to you. Have fun, experiment.

Exercise XI
PRIME THE PUMP

As human beings we are capable of the remarkable emotion of gratitude. Remarkable, because the simple act of appreciation has far reaching, positive consequences. What you focus on grows. In this exercise, you prime the pump of your dreams by appreciating and focusing on the things you enjoy in your life, the things that are working.

To begin this process, simply make a list of things for which you are grateful. The list might start with things like electricity, hot water, running water, a body that works—eyes that can see, legs that can walk, ears that can hear, or a stomach that can digest—a friend, the telephone, a job. How often we overlook so many things which we take for granted everyday. Allow yourself, as you begin this exercise, to take nothing for granted, and appreciate everything.

You may decide to make an evening review part of your daily ritual. At bedtime you can write out the things, events and people for which you feel grateful.

As gratitude becomes a more prominent feature in your life, you can pepper your day with appreciative thoughts—thanking the universe for the little moments, that happen everyday, that warm your heart.

The simplicity of this exercise belies its potency.

Exercise XII
MAY I HELP YOU?

We are meant to leave our little patch of garden in better shape than we found it. The old adage "when you give, you get" is as true as it is simple. We receive tenfold when we freely offer the universe what we have to give.

You have different gifts to offer the world at different times. Forcing yourself to give because you think you should creates toxic energy. But when you ask "what do I have to offer the world today?" you open the possibility as well as aligning yourself with your inner wisdom. Some days our gifts are simple—a smile, a flower to a colleague; other times our gifts seem grander—spending a weekend planting seedlings at a local park, helping build a house for a homeless family. The gift is not as important as the spirit in which it is given, for the true gift is our energy.

When you find yourself in a constricting situation with a stranger or a loved one, you may want to ask yourself "what can I do to help?" We are happier in all aspects of our lives when we can figure out how to keep the love within us flowing outward. That is our purpose in this lifetime.

INDEX

"Be really whole and all things will come to you." Lao-Tzu

If you'd like to sign up for Balloon: *the little newsletter with a lift*—Rhégina's free newsletter—you may do so by logging on to http://www.balloontothemoon.com.

Please address comments to Rhégina at
rhegina@balloontothemoon.com

BalloonToTheMoon.com

WHERE PEOPLE CULTIVATE THEIR DREAMS

ΑbreziaPress Quick Order Form

email orders: order@balloontothemoon.com
online orders: http://www.balloontothemoon.com
telephone orders: call 1.800.223.3242 toll free (credit card orders)
postal orders: Abrezia Press, PO Box 8129, Silver Spring, MD 20907

item	price	quantity	total
Balloon to the Moon: a Guide to Vibrant Living	$12.95 x	_____	= $_____
Balloon to the Moon audio-book; unabridged; read by author (approximately 3 hours)	$24.95 x	_____	= $_____
Subtotal			= $ ____
Shipping and handling (priority mail): U.S.: $4.00 for first book or audiobook, $2.00 each additional item; International: $8.00 first book or tape set, $4.00 for each additional item			= $ ____
Total:			= $ ____

Method of Payment:
❏ check or money order (made out to Rhégina Sinozich, MSW)
❏ MasterCard   ❏ VISA   ❏ Discover ❏ American Express

Credit Card Information:
card number: __ __ __ __ __ __ __ __ __ __ __ __ __ __ __ __

_____   _____
expiration date   authorized signature (as shown on credit card)

Name: _____
Address: _____
City: _____ State: _____ Zip:_____
Daytime phone: (   ) _____email:_____

YOUR NAME AND IDENTIFYING INFORMATION WILL
NEVER BE SOLD OR SHARED WITH ANYONE <u>PERIOD</u>.

BalloonToTheMoon.com

WHERE PEOPLE CULTIVATE THEIR DREAMS

AbreziaPress   Quick Order Form

email orders: order@balloontothemoon.com
online orders: http://www.balloontothemoon.com
telephone orders: call 1.800.223.3242 toll free (credit card orders)
postal orders: Abrezia Press, PO Box 8129, Silver Spring, MD 20907

item	price	quantity	total
Balloon to the Moon: a Guide to Vibrant Living	$12.95 x	_____	= $_____
Balloon to the Moon audio-book; unabridged; read by author (approximately 3 hours)	$24.95 x	_____	= $_____
Subtotal			= $ ____
Shipping and handling (priority mail): U.S.: $4.00 for first book or audiobook, $2.00 each additional item; International: $8.00 first book or tape set, $4.00 for each additional item			= $ ____
Total:			= $ ____

Method of Payment:
❑ check or money order (made out to Rhégina Sinozich, MSW)
❑ MasterCard   ❑ VISA   ❑ Discover ❑ American Express

Credit Card Information:
card number: __ __ __ __ __ __ __ __ __ __ __ __ __ __ __ __

_____   _____
expiration date   authorized signature (as shown on credit card)

Name: _____
Address: _____
City: _____ State: _____ Zip:_____
Daytime phone: (   ) _____email:_____

YOUR NAME AND IDENTIFYING INFORMATION WILL
NEVER BE SOLD OR SHARED WITH ANYONE <u>PERIOD</u>.

BalloonToTheMoon.com

WHERE PEOPLE CULTIVATE THEIR DREAMS

AbreziaPress Quick Order Form

email orders: order@balloontothemoon.com
online orders: http://www.balloontothemoon.com
telephone orders: call 1.800.223.3242 toll free (credit card orders)
postal orders: Abrezia Press, PO Box 8129, Silver Spring, MD 20907

item	price	quantity	total
Balloon to the Moon: a Guide to Vibrant Living	$12.95 x	____	= $_____
Balloon to the Moon audio-book; unabridged; read by author (approximately 3 hours)	$24.95 x	____	= $_____
Subtotal			= $ ____
Shipping and handling (priority mail): U.S.: $4.00 for first book or audiobook, $2.00 each additional item; International: $8.00 first book or tape set, $4.00 for each additional item			= $ ____
Total:			= $ ____

Method of Payment:
❏ check or money order (made out to Rhégina Sinozich, MSW)
❏ MasterCard ❏ VISA ❏ Discover ❏ American Express

Credit Card Information:
card number: __ __ __ __ __ __ __ __ __ __ __ __ __ __ __ __

_____   _____
expiration date   authorized signature (as shown on credit card)

Name: _____
Address: _____
City: _____ State: _____ Zip:_____
Daytime phone: (   ) _____email:_____

YOUR NAME AND IDENTIFYING INFORMATION WILL
NEVER BE SOLD OR SHARED WITH ANYONE <u>PERIOD</u>.

BalloonToTheMoon.com

WHERE PEOPLE CULTIVATE THEIR DREAMS

AbreziaPress Quick Order Form

email orders: order@balloontothemoon.com
online orders: http://www.balloontothemoon.com
telephone orders: call 1.800.223.3242 toll free (credit card orders)
postal orders: Abrezia Press, PO Box 8129, Silver Spring, MD 20907

item	price	quantity	total
Balloon to the Moon: a Guide to Vibrant Living	$12.95 x	_____	= $_____
Balloon to the Moon audio-book; unabridged; read by author (approximately 3 hours)	$24.95 x	_____	= $_____
Subtotal			= $ ____
Shipping and handling (priority mail): U.S.: $4.00 for first book or audiobook, $2.00 each additional item; International: $8.00 first book or tape set, $4.00 for each additional item			= $ ____
Total:			= $ ____

Method of Payment:
❑ check or money order (made out to Rhégina Sinozich, MSW)
❑ MasterCard ❑ VISA ❑ Discover ❑ American Express

Credit Card Information:
card number: __ __ __ __ __ __ __ __ __ __ __ __ __ __ __ __

_____   _____
expiration date   authorized signature (as shown on credit card)

Name: _____
Address: _____
City: _____ State: _____ Zip:_____
Daytime phone: (   ) _____email:_____

YOUR NAME AND IDENTIFYING INFORMATION WILL
NEVER BE SOLD OR SHARED WITH ANYONE <u>PERIOD</u>.